Ripples

Dedication

Ripples is dedicated to all the friends who have
been with me during the tough times - and of
course my publisher, who has shown such faith,
but most especially to my husband Tony. When
the waters got rough, it was his love and strength
that held my head above the waves.
My very special gratitude to Garth Brooks - just
for being the man that he is.

"This author's direct experience of regression creates a gateway into an amazing 17th century existence. This fascinating account eclipses effortlessly into our present time. One senses that destiny will create a chance for these two souls to meet again. A wonderful book."

SUE JAMES (five times nominated for country music awards)

"Last year I had the pleasure of meeting Garth Brooks in Nashville, Such was the coolness and 'down-to-earthness' of the man, that within a few moments, I had completely forgotten that I was in the company of the world's biggest selling recording artist. The character in this book could quite easily be him in a former life."

BARRY UPTON (Recording artist and songwriter - recent chart hit - 5,6,7,8, by 'Steps')

"Where to begin I would not know. The effect that Garth Brooks has had on my life I could not put into words. Jenny's story has and it is truly remarkable. A hypnotic read, full of intrigue and surprise. A real pleasure."

DAVE KANE (Kane & Co)

"Having met the dynamic Garth Brooks several times, I feel that he and Ryan Fitzgerald share the same qualities of strength and determination to please and succeed … intriguing and stirring … "

HANNAH VALIZE (Music journalist)

"A superb and exciting read. A must for all Garth Brooks' fans. *Ripples* is a haunting and bittersweet love story of two souls bound together through time."

KEITH POWELL (country singer)

Jenny Smedley wrote *Ripples* at the age of 45. She was inspired to do so by a paranormal experience which revealed her past life to her. This experience has touched and changed every part of her life, like the ripples on a pond. Since the experience she has also become a successful songwriter. Her acclaimed song, *I'm Still Falling*, co-written with Barry Upton (formerly of Brotherhood of Man), has featured on a top ten album and also as a video on CMT.

Jenny lives in the beautiful English county of Somerset, with her husband Tony, her aspiring film director son, Phillip, and their two dogs, 'Ace' and 'Peri'. Ace has quite a claim to fame herself, having saved Jenny's life and been acclaimed for it in national magazines.

Ripples

by

Jenny Smedley

Third Floor Productions

ISBN 0-9533083-0-8

Typeset by Amolibros, Watchet, Somerset

Printed and bound by Professional Book Supplies,
Oxford, England

Chapter One

This is a true story. Whether you choose to believe it or not will depend on how much magic you allow to dwell in your soul.

When I woke up that morning it seemed to be just another ordinary day, another day when I would have to struggle to find a reason to get out of bed, such were my feelings of sadness and futility. But at that point I did not know that it was to be the day when a miracle would happen.

I was at the lowest emotional ebb of my life. During the previous couple of years I had suffered from short bouts of depression, but lately they had built to frightening proportions. There seemed to be a hidden tragedy deep inside my mind, something that filled me with intolerable sadness and unreasonable fear. It was at this point that a total stranger changed my life forever, and not in any way that I could possibly have imagined.

For the last few months all I had been able to see ahead of me was a steady downhill slide, with no ups to look forward to. There were many blessings I could have counted - my husband, who was and has always been the love of my life, a twin shadow who matches me in every way, a loving and successful son, and our beautiful house in the country. But these blessings seemed to be things I didn't deserve, and I had no sense of being a special person. So that morning I thought that the only things to look forward to during the coming day were normal mundane housewifely chores along with the inevitable realisation that my life was pointless.

The miracle took place that evening.

A few days earlier I had caught a glimpse of a TV advert featuring a song by an all-American Country singer, and my interest had been piqued. So when I saw that his up and coming concert was to be shown on TV, I decided to video it. I also told my husband, Tony, that I thought I would like the singer's new CD for my approaching birthday.

I watched the showing of the concert later that evening, and from the first few seconds I was transfixed, not only by the obvious talent, for this man had enough fire and passion in him to drive a dozen ordinary men. He had an aura of reckless energy, a power which was one minute tamed to portray emotional heart-rending lyrics, and the next released, in breathtaking, limb-threatening stunts. My immediate reaction was that he was undoubtedly, wonderfully crazy. And my thoughts up to this point seemed very normal. After all, he had millions of fans who felt the same way about him.

He was a very attractive man, very physical, but not the type I usually felt an instant attraction for.

The concert lifted my spirits right from the start, but there was a point when he looked directly into the camera. As I had recorded the concert on video, I was able to follow my instinct, which was to freeze the frame. My eyes met his through the rather crude

2

medium of television - and that was it. I was instantly filled with immense profound joy, happiness that was totally illogical and irrepressible. The black cloud that had been hovering over me vanished in an instant. Where did these feelings come from? I didn't understand this at all. From the depths of depression, in a split second, I suddenly felt as if I would explode with ecstasy. This inexplicable feeling stayed with me. I tried to analyse it - and him. He was the complete cowboy, Stetson, tight jeans and cowboy boots. He prowled the stage with a slow easy walk that spelled controlled, physical strength. OK, thousands of people in the packed auditorium obviously felt huge adoration for him too - but not the way I did. I had never felt like this before in my whole life. I had been a fan of the Beatles in the 60s, and screamed along with the best of them, but this was a totally different feeling. I experienced a strange mixture of huge relief from a deep pain coupled with euphoria, along with a measure of desire combined with a fierce protective instinct towards this man, this last being by far the strongest. It was very strange.

He was nothing like my husband, whom I love more than anything. Tony is tall, slim and wiry, quiet and unassuming, and perfect to me. This guy was tall but there the resemblance ended. He was powerfully built, and as for quiet - forget it! What seemed the strongest of his features to me were, of course, his eyes. They were true blue, honest and compelling, direct and challenging. The old cliché that the eyes reflect the soul sprang to mind unbidden. They were eyes I felt I would know anywhere.

I sat and watched the whole concert, unable to tear my eyes from the screen. But at the end, I shrugged mentally, accepted the joy in my heart as a puzzling gift, and returned to the real world. For even I had no idea at that moment that the effects on me of this singer, whom I now knew to be called Garth Brooks, had barely begun.

From that night, I began to rediscover the joys of making love with Tony - I felt young again. But it was not how you are perhaps imagining. My mind was not filled with fantasy - I knew exactly whom I was with, and it was my husband. I was just experiencing the fledgling seeds of my old zest for life returning, a matter which filled both Tony and myself with wonder. I felt empowered by a new emotional strength. My family could not believe the new lightness of spirit which surrounded me. Colours grew brighter and my mind grew clearer.

This carried on for some weeks. I got Garth Brooks' CD which I played every morning while I ate my breakfast. Somehow the sound of his voice reassured me and put me in the right frame of mind to tackle any problems.

Then after a while strange things began to happen. I would just involuntarily go into a quiet meditative state that would be followed by a huge inrush of emotional power and energy. Each time this happened I grew mentally stronger, while the happiness inside me became more stable. Then my experiences became even stranger. I would be resting my hand on something when, for a split second, another hand would appear superimposed over mine. I wasn't afraid, just comforted, because by then I knew that something very special was going on. I had the pictures from Garth Brooks' CD cover, and I was thus aware that it was his hand I was seeing - or one very much like it.

4

However, although all this was very comforting I did start to experience a feeling of restlessness, as if there were some action I should be taking, but I had no idea what that might be.

I decided to speak to a friend of mine who was very knowledgeable on all things supernormal, and I asked her if it were possible to have a psychic connection with someone on the other side of the world. She answered simply, 'Of course.'

'But,' I countered, 'what if I never met this person?'

'Well,' she responded, without hesitation, but gently, 'not in this life maybe.'

Not in this life? Then when?

Chapter Two

She obviously meant in a previous lifetime. While I mentally digested this thought, life carried on. I had always been very open-minded about spiritual things, and I had begun to believe in reincarnation anyway, but I had never actually contemplated taking these thoughts further.

Like most of us, I was brought up to believe that if I always tried to do the right thing, I would go to heaven when I died. Only nowadays that doesn't quite cut it for me anymore. After all, God is supposed to be fair and just, but how, for instance, can a street kid in Calcutta, with no family, no home, and no food, possibly compete fairly in the 'being good' stakes with the average privileged Western child? However, by allowing for reincarnation the whole equation changes. The theory is that each time you die, you are shown the whole picture - where you have been before, and where you are aiming for spiritually. Then you get to choose the most appropriate next life in order to help you progress up the spiritual ladder. And, at the time, because you know the whole story, you choose the right next life, and not necessarily the nicest next life.

This theory does not negate the existence of God for me at all, in fact it confirms it. Besides, a lot of people don't realise that reincarnation was apparently mentioned widely in the Bible until it was taken out by the Romans - for their own purposes.

The other point that the concept of reincarnation makes sense of is the problem that if everyone who ever existed were a separate soul then heaven would be very crowded! Then follows another problem for we are also told that we will be with all our loved ones. The difficulty is that all our loved ones will also have all their loved ones, and their loved ones will have all their loved ones, and so on. We might not get along with all of them! So this is beginning to sound a little hellish to me! Now the theory of incarnation - well, the way I see it - is that we don't go to heaven or hell but we do progress, when our souls are ready and have learned enough, to the next spiritual level. Where or what that might be, I'm afraid I have no idea!

Strange and fantastic things continued to happen. I received what I can only call a vision of what I knew to be Garth's family's home in America, and described it in detail to my friends. This was very strange because Garth, whilst being a king in the Country Music scene, was not particularly well-known in England, and information on him was not easy to come by. However, eventually I tracked down a book about him, and no one was more surprised than me when an aerial photograph showed the exact same house I had described.

I thought these flashes of energy were enough but the influence of this special person hadn't ended yet. I had been a published poet for some while but I hadn't found it especially satisfying. I needed a new passion - and suddenly inspiration struck. What about song lyrics! I began at once. Within a few months I had amassed over two hundred sets of lyrics, so inspired was I. I used my initiative and found compatible composers to work with. Much to my amazement and to everyone around me, the song-writing started to take off, small steps at first but definitely steps in the right direction. This was wonderful and very fulfilling, yet I still felt something was missing from my life. My subconscious was calling out for me to do something but I wasn't sure what.

I struggled with this for several months. If I had known this man in a past life, what had he meant to me? Why had the very first sight of him triggered such powerful emotions in me? Who had he been? Who had I been? On the one hand I could try to establish contact with this person while on the other maybe I should just safely savour the feeling of 'coming home' that I experienced whenever I saw his face. For how could I know if I might like what I found out if I pursued this past life? My days were so much more pleasant now, so long as I saw his face at some point during each and every one. Of course a part of me wanted contact, though I knew this man wasn't going to play an intimate part in my present life. He was happily married, and so was I, besides, in this lifetime I was quite a bit older than him. However, I knew that he was one of those special people, who carry a 'secret flame' in their hearts - one of those rare and special people who seem to become rarer as we get older, a person who would share my wavelength and care for the same things as I did. He would be someone I couldn't help but love, and I would inevitably also love those close to him. It was like being kept apart from a much cherished friend.

For, as we get older, friends like this become the most important things in the world to us - people who can share all of our joys without ulterior motive, and who always have time to comfort us in moments of personal tragedy while keeping our confidences. But this was a very famous person. Someone in his position, especially a family man, needed to be surrounded by a defensive forest of people, whose specific task was to keep unknown hoards away from him; which, sadly, also meant that it kept away people who could be genuine friends - a bit like the way drift nets catch not only legitimate prey like tuna but also inadvertently catch precious dolphins too.

But still I didn't understand it. It is obvious to anyone that this man is unusually compassionate and passionate, but I didn't really know him as a person. And yet I *did* know him. I trusted him instinctively, without any doubts at all. I knew him to be emotionally vulnerable. I knew also that he would protect and defend his family with his life - no question. He is a person who, because of his huge talent and popularity, has been given enormous power, and yet I knew that he was someone who would never abuse that power, never trample over a 'little person' to get his own way. I knew he was very intelligent, quick thinking and quick acting, and someone who appreciated his life with an enthusiasm that made him dazzling to those around him. How did I know these things, for I had one hundred per cent belief in them? And, the biggest question of all: I'd lost touch with all the dreams in my life, I'd almost felt that my life was over, and yet this man, whom I'd never met, had lifted my spirits from the dark depths of the earth up into the stratosphere in one second of unconscious recognition; music of his kind lifts the spirits, but not to this impossible extent; what was going on?

I was told by my friend that some people believe that a past life's soul-mate will sometimes re-enter our lives briefly in times of crisis to try and redirect us onto our lost pathway. Maybe that was the answer, maybe he was a soul-mate. She also told me that a lot of people mistakenly confuse the term soul-mate with sexual partner. That is by no means always the case. Soul-mates can appear in their different incarnations as sons, daughters, lovers, brothers, or in any other relationship to us. But whomever they appear as, they are always the most special people we know. Some people, like me, are lucky enough to be married to a soul-mate, for that is the ultimate relationship, as I know. Tony and I have always known that we were soul-mates, ever since the very first moment we met.

I thought that maybe I knew a way to find the answers I needed. I was told about past-life regression under hypnosis. I had never been hypnotised, but I was getting desperate. I researched the classified phone book, and after chatting to several hypnotists, I chose a lady I seemed compatible with and who had done the same kind of thing before. But still I didn't make an appointment; it seemed so drastic. But as the next couple of weeks went by, my subconscious worried at the idea, like a dog with a rat, and eventually I found myself picking up the phone and arranging to see her. Tony took me, which was just as well as things turned out. I was in no fit state to drive afterwards.

I didn't know what to expect, but the lady assured me that she would only take me to happy memories.

I was soon sitting relaxed and she put me into a light trance. She then reawoke me, having suggested to me that I would go deeper next time. Twenty minutes later I was well under. Hypnosis is a difficult state to describe. If you have ever been able to make sense of those 3D pictures, you may understand. In just the same way that you see them when your eyes kind of jump out of focus, your brain slips into another sense when you are hypnotised. You are not asleep, and you are aware of what is being said. It is like a waking dream; thoughts and visions parade through your mind, and once you start talking, you find memories you didn't know you had coming back to you.

She first took me back through my present life, and I was able to recall tales of my infancy - later confirmed by my family. For instance I remembered falling in a neighbour's pond when I was three years old. I was able to describe the dress I was wearing. I also remembered the first time I walked, and I got very giggly because I thought that at last I would be able to catch the pet tortoise which roamed the garden. Then I regressed into the womb, and once again felt that peaceful, semi-sentient floating state.

Next I emerged through a mist into bright sunshine. In this life I was astonished to discover that I had been a man. I was a monk called Patrick in Italy in 1714. The hypnotist asked the question I had primed her with. 'Is the person you know as Garth in this lifetime with you?' The story was revealed but not in the way anyone expected. He had been my younger brother, and I hadn't seen him since we had been separated as young children. This discovery of having been a man, and a monk, was strange enough, but what happened next shocked the hypnotist to her roots. She told me afterwards

11

that control of me had been taken out of her hands, and that she was told what to say to me by a powerful third presence that she felt arrive in the room. She said that this had never happened to her before. She tried to take me back to the childhood of the monk, but I didn't go there. It seemed I had known an incarnation of Garth Brooks more than once.

Instead I emerged into the early morning sunshine of a day in the late spring of 1640. I was walking out of the confines of a garden into some woodland, and beside me was a man closely resembling a younger version of Garth. He looked a little different. Maybe his face was a little narrower, and his skin tone perhaps a shade darker, but there was no mistaking those eyes or that inner light. At this time he was also only about nineteen years old, although in those times people did look older than they do today. I felt no surprise at all at his being there, it seemed perfectly natural. I was female this time, and aged about eighteen.

We were walking hand in hand, he carrying a hawk that he had found injured and nursed back to health. We were going out to release it. We were so happy. The air vibrated with it. The hypnotist asked me to describe the house where we lived, and I will quote the narrative from here as if spoken by Madeleine Fitzgerald, as I was then called.

'The house is called ***** House [the name of the house has been witheld to safeguard the privacy of the current owners], and is red brick with black leaded windows. It is very large, and stands on a slope overlooking the village of Hambledon in the New Forest. [Hambledon actually exists in Hampshire and lies in a valley. I had never heard of it before. Interestingly, as Madeleine, I pronounced it Hamb-lee-don.] We live with my parents in the family house. My husband's name is Ryan. My parents have never approved of Ryan, coming as he does from common Irish stock, and he has never been considered as good enough for their daughter. I care nothing for their thoughts. We met when I was fourteen and Ryan fifteen. We ran away and were wed in secret when we were almost sixteen and seventeen. [This marriage took place on twenty-seventh April 1638.] We then returned to face my parents.

'They were beside themselves with anger. From that day, although they provide for us, we are not allowed in the family rooms, having "disgraced" their name. We are only allowed in our bedchamber, and the kitchen. We spend most of our time, when the weather is clement, outside. [During my provision of the description of the house, I saw the stairway as having metal balustrades, and thought I must be wrong. However I have since discovered that wrought iron balustrades did become fashionable at that time.] Our bedchamber is our refuge. It is quite dark, being panelled in wood, but made cosy by an all-year round fire. The bed is a four-poster, but not pretty or swathed in fabric. It is heavily carved and made entirely of wood. The mattress is very deep and soft, and the covers rough and woolly. The sheets and coverlet are heavy white material [like coarse cotton]. In the room there is a large bear. [This wasn't a real stuffed bear, but it looked quite real, unlike a teddy bear.] There is also a favourite doll of mine from childhood.

'The other room we are allowed in is the kitchen. This room is very large, with an enormous rectangular table in the middle. Around the walls and from the ceiling, which are plain plaster, there hang dozens of black tools and pots and pans. There is a door to the outside in the far wall. There is always a fire burning, and Ryan loves it in here because there is always food available and Nancy the cook, who loves us both, is a dear friend.

'Today is a beautiful day in May, in the year of 1640. It is still early, and the trees ahead are swathed in a ground mist so that it appears that we are about to wade through a waist-high sea. As the sun rises it filters through the trees, glinting on each droplet of water that dangles from the leaves, turning each one into a bright crystal of fire and ice. As I look back to the lawns of the garden, I can see the emerald trail our passage has created through the gossamer cobwebs that are strung across the grass. The trees, wreathed in skeins of ever shifting mist, stand in silent communion with each other.

'The darting movements of a deer cause the hawk's head to bob with interest, his eyes glittering. Ryan looks at the bird, and their eyes meet in apparent genuine communication. When we reach a small clearing, Ryan releases the hawk, and it alights on a branch, watching us. Ryan pushes me gently backwards against a tree trunk. I can feel its passive strength at my back. He pins me to the tree with his own body weight, and smiles down at me. He clasps both my hands in his, twining our fingers together, then stretching my arms out to the sides, and, leaning in, he kisses me. I can feel his passion growing against my skirts, and, illogically shy under the steady gaze of the hawk, I break away and run through the trees, laughing. I am dressed in a powder blue day gown, of shiny cloth. It is long, touching the ground at the back. It has a soft waist, and a large lace collar that turns down. My long, dark blonde hair is caught up in a pearled net and ribbons. My shoes are of a soft blue fabric and have silver decorations. Ryan is wearing a loose white shirt with a large collar. He has on a long black waistcoat and black breeches, laced below the knee. He has calf-length black leather boots. His hair is black and worn long, braided into a queue. [A queue is a pigtail.] We both wear plain wedding bands. [Madeleine also wore another gold ring - see later.]

'Ryan pursues me and catches me easily as we clear the trees, and he pulls me down in the long grass of the meadow. He is persuasive as always, the touch of his hands drawing an answering heat from me, despite the chilliness of the early morning air and the dampness of the dew. Time passes unnoticed by either of us. Our clothes are now dishevelled and my hair is loose. As we lie there resting in each other's arms I can see the hawk wheeling slowly overhead, a distant silhouette against the pure blue of the sky. My modesty was wasted after all.'

At this point, the hypnotist, who had promised at the beginning that she would only guide me to happy, trauma-free moments, found herself deviating from this, because, as she said later, she was instructed to do so by the mysterious third presence in the room. So she said, 'But something happened didn't it? Something happened to ruin your happiness. What went wrong?'

So my memories continued:

'Suddenly the mood is broken as we hear the frantic blowing of hunting horns coming from the house. Panicking at the thought of some dreadful disaster, we get up and begin running home. Halfway there, Ryan suddenly stops, and grasping my arm, stops me too. He does not want to go back, he senses danger. There has been talk of an

15

impending war with Scotland, and we have both feared that my parents may try and send Ryan to fight. But I assure him that it will be all right. Even if they have some scheme in mind, we will run away again - and this time we will not come back. Besides my father has been in ill-health for some time, and I am afraid the horns may have some morbid meaning, so we are going back.

'We know something bad is happening because we are summoned into the music room, and Ryan has never been permitted in there before. Now my parents are telling us that the king [I was amazed afterwards to discover that I had named the correct King for the period, for I was always a hopeless history student], Charles, is amassing an army to fight the Scottish, and - oh no - no! - dear God, no - they are saying that Ryan has to go - today - now! It cannot be true!

'We realise that some of my father's men have entered the room behind us, and at a signal from my father, the three of them roughly take hold of Ryan, two pinning his arms to his sides, and the third putting his arm around Ryan's throat from behind. My parents grasp my arms, but I struggle from their grip and clutch Ryan's hands, screaming at the men to let him go.

'Alas, my parents take hold of me again, and begin to prise our fingers apart. I cannot hold on to him! Oh my God, I cannot hold on to him!

'I cry out in terror, "Ryan! No! Ryan!" He struggles, but is pulled relentlessly backwards out into the hallway. His eyes meet mine despairingly. That last look will live with me forever, his eyes burning an image into mine. [And it did, tormenting me, causing bouts of depression for which I could find no reason, until I saw those same blue eyes on the TV screen. No wonder I was filled with such total joy when I saw them again. It was like a miracle.]

The door slams shut and I can hear Ryan shouting, the sounds of a fight, the dreadful sounds of blows. The noise dies away as I struggle and my father calls out for assistance. Two more men enter the room in response, and I am bundled upstairs and locked in a room. The walls of this small room are bare plaster, the door solid oak, and the only window is a narrow glassed slit. In desperation I lift a chair and smash the glass. The gap is too small to escape through. I can see the grounds below, and I cry out Ryan's name over and over again as I see him carried away, senseless, and then thrown bodily into the back of a wooden cart. The cart is driven away, and as I lose sight of it, and Ryan, I collapse to the floor , sobbing. My world is gone.

'I am sure that I will never see him again. I will never know what happens to him, and so my whole life has been totally destroyed in the space of a few minutes. I cannot believe it. As I look around the room, the full horror strikes. The room has been thoroughly prepared for this prisoner, with food and water enough for days! It was a despicable trick; Ryan did not have to go! My parents have finally betrayed us, as Ryan had always feared. I have been a fool. I cannot stand this pain…I shall go mad.'

Can you imagine how the trauma of the next two days and nights of Madeleine's imprisonment would have the power to affect me even today? If you are reading this you can surely envisage a loved one of your own being snatched from your arms by an enemy, and then finding yourself locked up, with no one to turn to, or even talk to, and all the while not knowing what fate is befalling the victim at the hands of that enemy. Imagine being unable to escape, and therefore unable to take any action, knowing that as the hours passed the chances of saving that person were also passing. It is amazing that Madeleine kept her sanity.

Some people have said that they are afraid of experiencing regression themselves. And, even more commonly, they say that they have enough problems in this life, without dredging up past life problems. But it is obvious to me, and I hope to you now, that most of their current problems probably started in a past life. Mine certainly did. I have great difficulty waiting even a few days for anything. It's no wonder, after that experience. Anyway, by now I was sobbing uncontrollably in the hypnotist's chair, and she began to try and soothe me, using words she was instructed to by the spirit in the room. She told me that love of this kind never dies, it goes on through the lifetimes, and that one day we would be together again. She brought me out of the trance. I felt completely gutted, drained, and cried out. The hypnotist looked pretty bad too. The experience had frightened her, I think. My husband was shocked when he saw the state of both of us. I collapsed into his arms, and thanked God he was there to take me home.

Naturally I felt compelled to find out the rest of the story. On further discussion with my psychic friend, I discovered that our subconscious has a spiritual guide (some people call them guardian angels), a guide that will steer us, when we're ready, to the scenes that we need to see, even if we don't realise that we need to. So this was the presence in the room that so shocked the hypnotist. She didn't seem at all keen to have me back, refusing to answer my letters, so I had to find another way.

Of course I was tormented by this memory - the appalling loss of someone I loved, and infinitely

18

worse, the knowledge that I never knew what happened to him. For Madeleine was right - she never saw him again. If I had expected anything from this regression, it would have been a gentle happy romance, not this nightmare feeling of total helpless despair that I felt now.

I found someone to teach me meditation, in order that I could use self-hypnosis. In this way you can ask questions of your spirit-guide, and as I discovered, find answers by being shown scenes you never actually experienced personally. And so with some trepidation I resolved to find out once and for all what had happened to Ryan after he was taken from me. I knew it wasn't going to be pleasant. The story unfolded this way.

Ryan was taken on board a ship which set sail immediately to an as yet unknown destination. Watched day and night, a prisoner, he was crudely trained in the use of a broadsword. (Again this proved to be the correct weapon for the time, although in this life I'm not sure I could even recognise one.) Then he was taken on board ship again, and it sailed for the east coast of England, somewhere around the area of Newcastle. By now it was midsummer, August 1640. On landfall they made their way inland to rendezvous with the English army of the King. But something went wrong, the army was not there. In confusion, this group of about fifty young men and the four officers decided to go back to the ship. But they were ambushed by a larger band of English soldiers, seasoned fighters, and they were brutally attacked. (I found this hard to understand at the time, but when we checked the history books later, we discovered that the first army Charles sent to fight the Scots, in August 1640, had mutinied, and had

19

formed into marauding bands, roaming the countryside, looting and pillaging. It must have been one of these bands of traitors that attacked them.) Ryan's group was all but destroyed, and almost weaponless now, forced to flee.

They managed to outrun the English soldiers, and with only about twenty left on their feet, some of whom were injured, they thought they had found sanctuary as they approached a small castle on a hillside. They advanced towards it cautiously, across a sparsely wooded slope. The grass was lush and green underfoot. Suddenly they heard the terrifying shouts and sounds of soldiers, coming from the trees on their right. It was the main advance of the Scottish army. Ryan was near the front of the group, and with the others who were unhurt, he turned to face the sounds, hoping that they might hold their ground long enough to allow the injured to make it to safety at the castle. Ryan carried only a shield. The army burst through the trees. The sight and sound was petrifying, even to me, an onlooker. There was an overall impression of reds and greens. Twisted, violent, painted faces, each one yelling blood-freezing war screams. They were awful in their ferocity. (I realised I was panting in extreme fear. What must it have been like for the men who actually had to face it?) And there were so many of them. I wanted to run. They had been brought to this bloodlust by weeks of frustrated searching in vain for the English army, and their screams were gleeful at having some Englishmen at their mercy at last.

(There is no doubt in my mind that, at this point, Ryan knew he was about to die. The only questions he could have asked were - how quick would it be and how painful? He could only have prayed for it to be quick for there was no hope of survival. The kind of courage it took for him to stand his ground is just impossible for me to comprehend.)

Like the others, Ryan was overwhelmed in the first wave. He tried to defend himself, but he was knocked to the ground by a numbing blow to his left arm, which was rendered useless. There was surprisingly little blood. As he hit the ground, the next soldier used both hands to thrust the full length of his broadsword through Ryan's abdomen. With indescribable horror, I saw the point of the blade glint red in the sunlight, as it emerged through his back. Now there was blood. So much blood. Ryan didn't scream as I expected. I hope his young mind had retreated into shock and couldn't be reached. As the blow struck he rolled onto his left side, curled around the hilt of the sword. The soldier lost his grip on the sword and ran on. Now that Ryan lay fatally wounded, I longed to touch him, and I reached out my hand towards him. His right hand gripped the hilt of the sword as if to hold it still, while his useless left arm lay with the hand palm up, fingers slightly bent. Poignantly, Ryan's hand displayed to me, in his dying moments, his exceptionally large mound of Venus, the fleshy pad of the thumb. This is meant to denote a passionate nature, as in Ryan's case it did. His fiery enthusiasm for life never failed to draw me in. Now that passion was about to be extinguished. I felt devastated. (I have not at this time been close enough to Garth to see the undersides of his hands, but I have no doubt they have the same feature.)

As I looked into his eyes they turned dreamy and far away, and I pray that he felt no pain. I could barely continue to watch, but I wanted to know the end for sure, so I still saw him as he drew ever

21

shallower breaths. He never moved again, and it seemed like forever he lay there barely breathing, with just an occasional deep moan.

As time passed, and Ryan lay dying before my eyes, I felt my life-force also slowly draining from my soul, leaving an empty ache behind it, an ache that I believe will only now be soothed, by remembering this past life, and by resolving after three hundred years or more, the mystery of what happened to him. Finally his breathing turned to gasping, and then mercifully stopped. How truly awful it was, to be forced to be grateful for the dying breath of someone I knew I could not live without.

At least I know what happened to him now, even if as Madeleine I never did, not for sure. She never spoke to her parents again. They really thought she would get over it in time. They were wrong. The part of me that will always be Madeleine has mourned Ryan for over three hundred years.

From the day I saw this vision, I have been unable to watch anything realistic involving fighting with broadswords. The much acclaimed film, *Braveheart*, was in the cinemas at the time, but the thought of seeing similar ferocious faces to those I saw that day, inflicting similar atrocious injuries, filled me with a sense of dread.

Poor Madeleine never saw these scenes in her lifetime. How dreadful that I lived the rest of that life, never knowing what happened to Ryan. It really is the 'not knowing' that destroys you. When it was first suggested to me that I incorporate these memories into a novel, it seemed a little too personal, but on reflection I realised it was probably the only way, not only to expunge the past, but to provide a fitting memorial to Ryan. Personally I now read

22

history with a new sensation. When I read of past deeds and particularly terrible injustices I understand that these historical figures were real people, with real feelings, just like you and me. In fact they may have actually been you or me.

Chapter Three

At this point life became very difficult for a while. I began mourning in earnest, something I had never really been able to do as Madeleine, for, from the moment he was out of their sight, her parents denied Ryan's very existence. I would be walking around the supermarket for instance, shopping on automatic, when I would suddenly be overcome with the vision of Ryan's terrible death. I have always had a morbid dread of swordplay, feeling that there is nothing so horrifying as being hacked to death - such a slow and agonising end to a life. Now I knew why. I have also always had a lifelong bad feeling about Scotland, never able to really enjoy its spectacular scenery, or tolerate the idea of living there. I saw scenes, not long after this, of Northumberland and the area around Hadrian's Wall, on a travel programme. The grass was the very same pea-green as the grass around the castle, and I felt so physically sick that I had to leave the room.

However the grief slowly subsided to a background level, and I felt strong enough to delve into more details of my previous life. This, I feel was almost solely due to the love and support I received from Tony. His understanding and acceptance of the situation astounded me. I wanted to know the whole story of Ryan and Madeleine's love. I felt I had seen the worst part, and I hoped for some more pleasant recollections. I wanted to know more about Ryan's personality. I knew without doubt that Madeleine had loved him dearly, but I wanted to know him completely, and myself too. I also felt that by learning more about Ryan, I would inevitably be learning more about Garth too. But sadly, there was yet more trauma to come before the memories became gentler. Madeleine takes up the narrative.

Late May 1640 (One week after Ryan's abduction)

'I feel almost insane. Nancy, the cook, the only other person in the household who loved Ryan, is my only saviour. My parents tell me I will get over it, that it is all for the best and that now they can find me a husband worthy of the family. Worthy! Oh God! Ryan was worth any ten of them! I loathe them with all my heart. If they try to make me marry, I will refuse. They do not know what has become of Ryan any more than I do. We have had no news. Even if they could show me his body [I cry even now at the thought], I would rather kill myself than let any other man ever touch me. I wish I was with his child, but even then I would fear that evil pair would kill it as soon as it was born. Will this pain never end…

'Nancy does her best to comfort me, but we end up crying in each other's arms, both of us longing for the arms of another. Never to hold him again - if only I knew Ryan's fate - where is he? Sometimes it becomes too much for me, and I become hysterical, screaming and running through the house, breaking things. The household is beginning to look at me as if I am mad. I do not care, nor do I care if I die. Sometimes I wish I would - maybe I will make it so. But the only thing that holds me back, is just supposing I ended this foul existence, and by some miracle Ryan returned. I am sure he will not but the thought is too dreadful to contemplate.

'Sometimes I sit for hours beneath our tree [where they kissed], and sometimes I try to find the place where we lay in the meadow. I lie there alone, trying to scent Ryan in the long grass which now seems yellow and sour. They destroyed all of Ryan's belongings, even his writings, while I was still a prisoner, saying it was for my own good, but I fear they have left my sanity nothing to cling to.'

Naturally these kind of regressions make me very upset, and I have to leave it for a couple of days, until I feel strong enough to continue. I decided to try a different direction for a while, and I wanted to find out how we first met. This is what I discovered.

'I was only fourteen, and out riding alone, something I had been forbidden to do, when my horse threw me. I hit my head and was knocked senseless. When I awoke, to my horror I found my clothes were in disarray, and my skirts had ridden high, exposing my bare legs. I hurriedly covered myself, and then became aware of a furious tussle taking place between three lads. One seemed to be fighting the other two. He was very strong, and within minutes both of the other ruffians had taken to their heels.

'The remaining lad hurried back to me. I was terrified! Had he won the opportunity to use me for himself? He threw himself to his knees at my side. I flinched, scrambling away from him. His eyes lifted to mine, and he looked offended.

'"My Lady," he protested, "I would never hurt you. Indeed I have just seen off those who would have done you harm." His voice was a soft Irish brogue, and his eyes - well, suffice it to say that I had no fear of him from that moment, in fact I believe love was there from that very first second. [I break in here to say that I had the same experience with my present husband - not the threatened rape - but the instant love. His eyes are brown, not blue, soft and expressive, genuine, and capable of pulling you in, and of seeing right through to your soul. His eyes also met mine with an almost audible click, forever linking us in spirit. I would also add that at this time Ryan was very thin, having barely escaped starvation in Ireland. It also made sense to me at this point, that while most people's regressions may reveal a violent death that is haunting their spirit, for me it would always have been emotional violence that left its mark.]

'Ryan Fitzgerald, as I discovered the young man's name to be, had been born in Ireland, and had worked his shipboard passage, landing at Southampton. And now he was trying to work for his keep in England. He had no baggage, only the clothes he stood in. I resolved to take him back home to my parents, hoping in truth that he would stay, for I felt drawn to him in some way. But as we approached the road we were met by a party of my father's farm workers coming to search for me, since my horse had returned alone. Taking one look at my torn gown, and muddied appearance, they leapt to the wrong conclusion, and bore Ryan to the ground. Thank the Lord, they finally listened to my pleas of protest before they had damaged him too greatly. They still, however, continued to view him with some suspicion as we made our way home.

'I could not believe the behaviour of my parents. They were only coldly grateful to Ryan, and seemed to want rid of him as soon as possible. I left him in the kitchen with Nancy, who seemed to take an instant maternal shine to him, and proceeded to stuff him with food. Then I confronted my parents and demanded an explanation for their rudeness. I was treated like an erring child, and told that this lad had seen me at a disadvantage and could not be trusted to keep quiet about it; that, anyway, they only had my word for it that he had not taken advantage of my senseless state, and I had been confused by the blow to my head. I refused to accept their counsel on this matter. I did not care what they said, Ryan was staying.

'Things got worse as time went on, and my parents could see that Ryan and I were becoming closer and closer. For my part I had never known anyone like him. He said things that should have come from a much older person, and he showed a compassion rare in young men. He truly delighted me. Then one night I overheard my parents discussing ways to persuade Ryan to leave. They decided to offer him a large sum of money if he would go. I knew Ryan well enough by then to know that this would incense him, and that he would finally lose all respect for them. [It was on that very night that Ryan asked Madeleine to marry him and they planned their secret elopement.]'

I was quite surprised that, given their obvious disapproval, Madeleine's parents allowed them to go to her bedchamber alone, after they had confessed to their secret marriage. When I meditated on it, I came up with two possible reasons. First, they may have assumed it was too late, for they would not have believed that Ryan would have waited for marriage before he slept with Madeleine, and perhaps in their shock they had just let events continue till they thought about what to do next: or, second (and I believe this is the right reason), because they had tried to turn Madeleine against Ryan on many occasions and had never come close to succeeding, they were banking on their belief that he was nothing more than a common lout, and that a single night in his bed, and in his depraved company, would have an innocent like Madeleine screaming to be rid of him. They couldn't have been more wrong.

'Surprisingly, Ryan had not bedded me before our marriage, although we had come very close to it. When we were alone in my bedchamber, Ryan gave me this verse that he had penned:

> Two rivers flowing into one, now our
> journey has begun
> Carried helpless on the tide, heart to heart
> as we ride.
> We soar up like birds of prey, turning night-
> time into day
> Stretching up to meet the sky, flying where
> the eagles fly.
> They say our love cannot be, as we sail into
> the sea.
> They try to tear us apart, they cannot see
> we are one heart.

I had never delved too deeply into his past, but I knew that even at his young age, I was not his first bed-mate. I did not mind, this helped me in fact, for

29

it meant that he did not rush at me like a raging bull, as I had heard tell other men did. Older women, already married, had warned me of these men, although I confess that I had not always comprehended these warnings. I had no knowledge at all of the bodies of men. Some of the women had told me that they had been shy of their marriage bed ever since the first night. But when Ryan took me it was different.

When we were alone in my bedchamber, my thoughts were abounding with joyful anticipation, but there was also a little fear. Nancy and Sarah had made me somewhat concerned by their talk of being hurt by an impatient man. I had not comprehended their meaning at all. But soon I realised what they had meant. I need not have worried however. Ryan treated me with gentleness and extreme patience; assuring me that there was no need to hurry. He did not enter me until I was more than ready to receive him, and at that very moment, when I did feel some fear, he deliberately smiled down at me and held my gaze, so that I knew he would not hurt me. My abiding memories of that night, however, were twofold. When Ryan first gazed upon my naked body, his eyes and his respectful manner gave me a feeling of great power over him. To feel such power over one so strong was not something I had ever expected. The other surprise was the pleasure he gave to me. No woman had ever spoken to me of the pleasure a man could give a woman, were he considerate enough. Sadly for them, I think that they never experienced this pleasure in their marriage beds. As for myself, Ryan gave me so much ecstasy that I though I might die from it. When I awoke to his kiss in the early hours, I felt nothing but welcome for his attentions. Nothing was more joyous to me than having his hands touch me. There was heavy rain pounding against the windows, but I felt so safe and warm in the comfort of his arms. My love for him after that night reached new dimensions. To have a man such as this was surely every woman's desire.'

Chapter Four

Now I felt that I knew most of the story. I still have new memories, and I will tell you these as they occur. But I was left with my true dilemma. Imagine my pain. I had rediscovered this wonderful man, alive again, but out of my reach. I had a deep, almost obsessional need to see him again with my own eyes. I know Garth is with the right woman for him in this lifetime, as I am with the right man. I would never be cut out to be married to a big star anyway as it requires too much strength.

But I ask you to imagine my feelings. I can only liken it to hearing that someone you love has had a bad accident. Even if people told you he was OK, you would still need to see him with your own eyes. Now imagine that you thought someone you loved was dead, lost to you forever, and then you were told it was a mistake. Think how you would need to see this person for yourself, both to see he was really OK and to make sure he was not about to disappear again. This was what I needed. If I could ever physically touch him, so much the better. Even if he didn't recognise me - it wouldn't matter. We are not all ready at the same time to face our past. I wouldn't necessarily expect him to be able to accept my story. I just needed to see him.

However, this is where the problems really began. Garth is a very famous man, surrounded as they all have to be by a barrier of people. To them, to him even, I was nothing more or less than one fan amongst millions, all trying to get close to their idol. Why couldn't he have just been an ordinary man in the street? - although the snag with that is that I might, of course, never have seen him had he not appeared on TV. There was no way I could write and tell him of my knowledge, even if he were open to such things, because any mail had to go through a fan club. And obviously, any strange letter would be trashed as cranky, without him ever having seen it. I couldn't leave it. I had to find a way to try. Without the completion that would result from seeing him, I didn't think I would ever get over it. Mind you, I didn't know what might happen, should I ever come face to face with him. Eye to eye with Ryan again! Just imagine!

Some of the weird things that happen when your spirit is opened to possibilities had begun to happen to Tony and I. He was always very supportive, by the way, of my efforts to meet Garth, knowing as he did, the huge spiritual uplift I had gained from the present tenuous contact. And he was content that there was no threat to our relationship. Besides, we had both brought crystals to wear, to enhance our psychic abilities, and we had discovered that when he was away on business, we could maintain a contact. For instance, I would always know what time his plane was going to land, and was there to meet him, even when it was thirty minutes early. And once, I had even described to him a room he had a meeting in, although I had never seen it.

However, I couldn't send a psychic message to Garth because it seemed that I could only receive messages, and not send them.

Some people poke fun at the idea of crystals affecting us in any way. But it is actually quite logical. Scientists agree that our brains send messages throughout our bodies by electrical impulses. Therefore, like any electrical device, we must have a magnetic field, or aura, as I call it. Crystals are not just any old lumps of rock either. They too have electrical properties. They were used in ancient Egyptian batteries, and today, in transistors, and even silicon chips. Therefore, if our field, or aura, is out of balance in some way, why shouldn't the insertion of the correct crystal have a beneficial effect on us?

Seeing Garth at a concert was a possibility, but such events mostly took place in America. Then as the seats for his concerts usually sold out in less than an hour, getting seats from the UK was almost impossible. Besides, I had never travelled on a plane. I'd had a lifelong phobia of air travel, and even my brother, who is a qualified pilot, had never been able to get me in one. There was supposed to be an upcoming concert in England, but that was possibly a year away. Too long to wait. Tony had quite given up, after twenty-five years, trying to persuade me to go abroad for a holiday, but now I astounded him. How about - I said - going to America for a holiday? Stunned silence! One of the changes that have been wrought in me since rediscovering Ryan is a new courage, a taste for life. That the chosen destination was Nashville - where Garth lives - was no real surprise, however! But the problems didn't end there. This man was on tour currently, and even if he was there and I was able to direct us to his home, we could hardly just knock at the door, and expect a warm reception.

Someone in Nashville, with inside information, had offered to get me the name of the hospital where their new baby was to be born to his wife Sandy, so that I could waylay him en route. But that wasn't the sort of thing I would ever do. This was a man I had loved deeply, more than life itself - and I still did in a way. I would defend his rights always. And I would never ever do anything to hurt him, or cause him to look at me with any animosity. I couldn't have handled that at all. I knew there was very little chance that he would be ready to recognise me, but at least I wanted him to know that I was a nice person.

Madeleine has described Ryan as behaving in a way that was much older than he was. This is a memory of an occasion when he showed this kind of behaviour.

August 1639 (sixteen months after their wedding)

'Sarah, Nancy's sister, arrived at the house today in a terribly distraught state. She and her daughter, Emily, worked in the Chalfont household. Emily was but twelve years old, and something truly awful had happened to her. She had been assaulted by the Chalfonts' son, James. This had put Sarah in a dreadful position, as well as upsetting her so dreadfully. For had Sarah reported this disgraceful act, she would have lost her position, she would have lost her home, and she would have become unemployable.

'James Chalfont (aged twenty-two), had come across Emily in the dairy, after milking had ended, and where she was scrubbing the churns. No-one else had been abroad. James had cornered her, and after battering her quite badly when she had resisted him, he had torn her clothes and he had raped her. She had been a maiden. When Sarah came to us this day, it was two weeks after the wicked deed. It was the first opportunity she had found to get away from the estate. Naturally she had brought Emily with her, for she was afraid to let the child out of her sight. Poor Emily's face was still yellow and purple with bruising. But the worst thing, in Sarah's eyes, was that Emily was now totally terrified of all men, and could not bear any man near her. This made the future look very bleak, not only in the workplace, for most employers would be men, but Emily was very pretty, and Sarah had enjoyed high hopes of her marrying well. Emily had been so badly hurt and abused, that Sarah feared she would never recover enough to live a normal life.

'I was very sympathetic but I did not know how to help her. Two hours later, the four of us were seated around the kitchen table, when Ryan came in from his work. I greeted him warmly, and only saw afterwards the result of James Chalfont's attack on Emily. For the poor child, at the sight of Ryan, who had certainly never done her any harm, became quite panic-stricken. She ran to her mother's side and huddled up against her, whimpering pitifully. Ryan knew nothing of what had transpired, but seeing her fear, he was careful to keep the table between himself and Emily, and did not look directly at her. He sat down with me, as was our custom, and ate his supper.

'I must explain that Ryan is very charismatic. And his very presence carries with it a feeling of power

36

and safety. I always feel safe when I am with him. So after a while, I think because she felt some of this, and because Ryan did not look her way, Emily began to be calmer, and she sat down once more. By the time Ryan and I retired to our bedchamber, she began to smile a little but she was still careful not to look at him lest she attract his attention. When we reached our bedchamber, I explained to Ryan what had happened to Emily. He was incensed by this dreadful account. It was just one more example to him of how some people abused their positions of power, something which always made him angry. He felt awful about the fact that James Chalfont would go unpunished and uneducated as to other folks' rights in this world. Sarah was a widow, and Emily her only child, born to her late in life, was very precious to her. This was something James Chalfont would never understand. To him the likes of Emily were only there to serve his every desire, for he was, after all, superior to her. I was a little concerned that Ryan might decide to punish James Chalfont himself, and I later discovered that I had been right to be. Ryan went back down to the kitchen briefly to suggest quietly to Nancy that she persuade Sarah to leave Emily with her for a few days. No doubt some would be amazed at Sarah trusting Ryan with her child, but this was the effect he had on all good souls.

'So the next day Emily could be found clinging to Nancy's skirts wherever she went. That day, however, when Ryan came into the kitchen, Emily seemed a little calmer in his presence. And that day he even drew a slight smile from her in response to his. His smile has always been totally infectious. But still he made no attempt to speak to her or touch her.

37

'The following day Ryan disappeared for over three hours, and, when he returned to us where we sat in the kitchen, he walked over to Emily, moving slowly so as not to alarm her. She drew back slightly, but remained seated. Ryan gave her the most courtly of bows, sweeping his arm out to the side. Then he presented her with a posy from the garden which she took shyly.

'"My Lady Emily," Ryan began, "may I have a moment to speak with you?"

'I do not think anyone had ever addressed her this way before, and it surprised her so much that she forgot her fear for an instant.

'"Yes," she answered in a whisper.

'Ryan got down on one knee in front of her, lessening his size so as to retain her frail confidence in him. Then he reached out his hand very slowly, as if she were a nervous colt, and took her hand in his.

'"From this day forth, My Lady," he continued, "I shall be your champion. If you are ever under threat, call on me and I will defend you. Do not fear any man, for I will exact a fearful vengeance on any who cause you harm. Let everyone know that this be so."

'As a young girl, of course Emily had heard tales of brave Knights of old and their fair Ladies, and so this romantic Knight-like turn of phrase went straight to her heart.

'Ryan continued, "As for My Lady's sworn enemy, James Chalfont," Emily flinched slightly at the mention of his name, and gripped Ryan's hand tighter, "he is now also my own enemy, and this he knows. He knows that he dare not ever harm My Lady Emily, for my revenge against him would be swift and sure. Have no more fear of him for he is a coward and a scoundrel."

'Emily smiled delightedly. To her, a girl-child without a father, the notion of having a sworn protector must have been very reassuring.

'When we retired, I asked Ryan what had transpired. He had, as I had suspected, confronted James Chalfont, and the bully had been bullied. Ryan had tried to talk to him in the first instance, and point out to him the error of his ways. But like most bullies, Chalfont only understood one thing - violence. So Ryan had given up trying to save his soul, and had subjected him to a humiliating experience instead. It was obvious that Chalfont was a coward, from his attack on poor defenceless Emily, and Ryan had reduced him to pathetic tears, merely by his physical threat and by pushing him bodily up against a wall. I was not surprised at Ryan being able to do this, for I had seen him before change in a split second, from a kitten to a tiger. His normally gentle-looking face could turn ferocious in an instant, totally surprising an adversary.

'The next day was a holiday, so we asked Emily to accompany us on a picnic. Her demeanour now was satisfyingly different, and she agreed with alacrity. During this outing Ryan won her over completely by treating her the whole time as if she were a Princess, lifting her carefully onto and off her horse, and fetching and carrying for her in a completely humble manner. And all day, Ryan deliberately made himself into a fool, crawling after her on his knees, until Emily even began to laugh at him.

'Then she found a path to real release. It was at a moment when Ryan was down on both knees in front of her, she playing the part of a fine lady - he the servant. She stopped play-acting the part, and went very still, as her eyes locked with his for the first time. She froze for an instant…then she threw her arms around his neck. She clung to him while sobs seemed to burst from the very centre of her soul, and she cried for the first time since the foul attack on her small person. Ryan wrapped his arms around her and held her, not like a baby, but like the fledgling woman she was, tenderly but with respect and strength. She cried until the tears had trickled down his neck and begun to soak the shoulder of his shirt. When she finally drew back it was with a tremulous smile, and I could see that at last her heart was soaring back into that childish realm of joy where it belonged for a little longer yet.

[Some might wonder if as Madeleine I felt any vestige of jealousy when Ryan gave so much of his attention to another. I can definitely answer no to this. Madeleine was extremely proud of Ryan at these moments. His behaviour at these times, and his compassion, only made her love him more.]

'When Sarah came to collect Emily that evening, she was astounded and grateful to find her standing next to Ryan where he sat, leaning comfortably against him, her arm companionably across his shoulders, and he with his arm about her waist. When they left, Emily said in parting, "Goodbye Sir Ryan, My good Knight."

'"Farewell, My Lady," Ryan responded, then made her giggle by adding, "May the days pass swiftly until my eyes behold your beauty once more."

'Most young men that I knew would have taken advantage of this sorry situation and, not caring about poor Emily's feelings, they would have made ribald remarks. They would have sniggered and whispered and been totally unable to put themselves in another's position. They certainly would have been incapable of helping her as Ryan had done.'

Writing the preceding account was a very strange experience: for I typed it directly onto the word processor without any prior thought and, as I was writing it, I had no idea what the next word would be, let alone the whole episode. I believe this kind of thing is called 'automatic writing'. It all came straight from my subconscious onto the page. All the time I was thinking that I couldn't wait to see what Ryan had done to rectify the situation.

You may also have noticed another strange phenomena about regressions. Sometimes I am inside Madeleine, seeing things directly through her eyes and feeling things directly through her emotions, while at other times the experience is almost like a film that I am watching.

It came to me now that this affinity with children was one of the things that made Ryan so special. Every child that ever met him saw, as children often do, straight through to his heart. And every child found there something that inspired in him or her instant trust and security. They sought him out instinctively at any sign of trouble, totally certain that he could, and would, help them without question. It sometimes seemed to me very sad that adults appeared to lose this ability to see the truth, or at least buried it beneath pride, ambition, and fear.

There follows a memory which displays another example of a child's justifiable trust in Ryan. It happened in September 1638, six months after Ryan and Madeleine's wedding.

'We knew nothing of the trouble that had befallen the Oswald family until the moment that Lucy, their seven year old daughter, burst in through the back door, and into the kitchen, sobbing, and incoherent. She dodged determinedly around Nancy's outstretched arms, past me as I tried to catch her, and around the table, throwing herself straight into Ryan's arms where he sat. She scrambled up onto his lap in an instant, and clung around his neck. Ryan stood up, carrying her, and he rocked her to and fro soothingly, talking to her all the while.

'"Lucy - Lucy - hush, hush now - what has happened?" She was unable to answer in her hysterical state. We needed to know what the problem was before we could begin to help, so Ryan lowered her feet to the floor, and knelt in front of her, but he could not prise her from himself. Still she held on to him, as if the very fabric of her world depended on it.

'Nancy and I had to intervene, pulling her arms from around Ryan's neck, and drawing her back, so that he could see her face, and she his. She struggled pathetically in our grip. Ryan placed his hands on her shoulders, gently restraining her.

'"Now," he began again, "Lucy, tell me what is wrong."

She focused on his face now, and her sobs decreased enough for her to speak between hitches. "Oh Ryan…please help us…Mama is hurt…they are going…to…to burn our cottage!"

'At this news Ryan and I made to leave immediately. But Lucy, whom we wished to leave in safety with Nancy, would not be taken from Ryan, and once more clung leech-like to him. So he picked her up again, and we made our best speed, praying we would not be too late to help. We ran through the gardens and the woods, down the meadow, and then left, into the lane at the bottom. By now, despite

42

his burden, Ryan had left me a little behind, hampered as I was by my long skirts. The Oswalds' cottage lay but a few hundred paces towards the village.

'The scene stood out in stark relief as I reached it. Dan Oswald lay on the ground, bleeding from a head wound. Peggy Oswald struggled in the arms of a man who was apparently a debt collector, and a second man, who held a flaming torch, was approaching the cottage with it, his intentions obvious. At our sudden appearance, everyone froze for an instant, assessing this change to the situation. Ryan moved first. He was still hampered, because Lucy would not let go of him but screamed in terror. So he ran with her to Dan, and pushed her towards him, saying, "Lucy, take care of your father!"

'Seeing Dan up close released her from her hysteria, and she transferred her attention to him. Ryan, now free to act, strode towards the torch-bearer. As I had seen happen before, Ryan's height advantage gave the villain pause, and Ryan was able to wrest the torch from him, and douse it in the thick dust of the yard, so alleviating the threat of fire for the moment.

'Then he quickly turned and walked purposefully over to the other man who held Peggy, and he said with deliberation, "Let her be."

'"This is no concern of yours," the man protested. "You would be best advised to be about your business, and leave us to deal with our own."

'"Ryan!" Peggy cried desperately, "We have the money! Dan has just returned from market with it!"

'"Silence woman!" the man yelled, shaking her roughly. "It is too late for that!" He glared at Ryan, "Be off with you!"

'Ryan merely repeated, "Let her be!"

'The man looked to his companion and then, without a word, he shoved Peggy from him and drew himself up threateningly. They were after all, he obviously thought, still two against one. Peggy fled to her family.

'I ran forward to stand at Ryan's side, hoping to avoid the violence, which hovered over the scene like an approaching storm.

'I addressed the man. "I am Madeleine Fitzgerald of ***** House," I said in my haughtiest manner, "and if it is found that you are acting without proper authority, you will pay dearly."

'"We have our orders," the man in front of us replied. "They cannot pay their rent, and we are to fire the cottage as a warning to others."

'By now Dan had come to his senses and he called out, "I have the owings here. I have tried to tell you!" Then he suddenly shouted, "Ware! Ryan! Behind you!"

'The man who had wielded the torch was coming towards Ryan from behind. It seemed my warning had not been heeded, and that they were determined to fight. Dan tried to come by way of assistance, but his wife had to support him as he almost fell, still dazed, for he had already been weak from ill-health before the blow to his head. The man in front snarled aggressively at us as his companion came at us from behind. Ryan swiftly pushed me away with his left arm and at the same time, with his right, he grasped the shirt of the man in front of him. Pivoting, he pulled this man around so that he collided with his cohort behind, and both of them fell to the ground, tangled together. Ryan made no further move, but merely stood over them, waiting to see what they would do next. Not needing to speak, they clambered up in a rush, angry and humiliated and

44

reaching for their tormentor. He side-stepped the first man who sprawled once more on the ground, and planted a heavy fist on the second man's nose which turned scarlet in an instant. This man sat down hard, and Ryan turned back to the first man who by now had regained his feet. Ryan took half a step towards him and the man backed off slightly, looking wary. Ryan stared at him for a few silent seconds.

'"Look," the man blustered, "we were only following our orders."

'It was plain that they had not expected much of a struggle from a sick man and his wife and child. Ryan did not answer. He walked over to Dan, and Dan silently handed him the money pouch containing the rent. Ryan retraced his steps, and pushed the pouch into the debt collector's hands.

'"Now," he said, "you have your money. You have no more business here. Go!"

'"I am a witness that you have been paid in full," I added for good measure. Ryan reached down and pulled the injured collector to his feet, and then pushed him away, so that he stumbled off in the direction of his partner. The two of them made off. More enemies for Ryan, I thought, as the men glanced back as if to be sure they would remember him.

[I am becoming aware that quite a few people, as well as Madeleine's parents, did not like Ryan. But these were always the same type of people. Often they did not like him because they feared him. They knew that he soured their schemes, and evil plots, because he interfered, as they saw it, in their business. He would not turn a blind eye and take care only of himself as most people did. Injustice to him, was like a red rag to a bull.]

'"How can we thank you?" Peggy and Dan wanted to know, "You have saved our home."

'Lucy had no doubt. She ran to Ryan and put her arms around his waist. "I knew you would help us," she said, smiling up at him. Ryan crouched, and hugged her in return, as she transferred her grip from his waist to his neck.

'Dan shook him by the hand, saying, "Thank you lad, we owe you a good deal."

'Peggy lifted her daughter from Ryan's arms, saying, "And thank you, Lucy. You had good enough sense to go to the right place for help. You are a good child."

'We returned home to appraise Nancy of the events, knowing that she would be anxiously pacing the kitchen, awaiting our return.'

Chapter Five

So at last I was beginning to have good memories - episodes from our lives together, reminding me of why and how much, as Madeleine, I had loved this rare and special person. Another such memory came to me in late March.

Eleventh May 1638

'It was one of those rare and special days when everything seems to be perfect. There was some magic in the air right from the early morning when we set off. There was a pearly, almost pink mist kissing the gardens. It gave me such a mystical feeling that I would not have been surprised to see a unicorn come prancing out of the dawn. Ryan and I had grown tired of listening to all the household (except Nancy of course) constantly criticising our young marriage, and we had planned this day of blissful escape. We left the house before anyone else had risen, except for a few servants. Nancy had, as she had promised, packed us a basket of food to take with us. We saddled our two favourite horses, Cherish, a golden coloured mare, and Fallow, a grey mare.

'We were excited at the prospect of a day alone together, exploring unknown reaches of the forest. We had only been married for two weeks. We rode for several hours until the sun rose high and began to make both us and the horses hot and sweaty. When we came to the clearing, we were almost speechless at the beauty of it. [I wonder if this clearing still exists. Sadly, the New Forest is much smaller today than it was originally.] At the foot of the slope in front of us ran a bubbling stream. It was crystal clear and ran deep in places over large rocks. We descended the slope and found that the rocks in one place had formed a natural pool which foamed and swirled as the water tried to escape from its confinement. There were some smaller trees here, young oaks and beeches struggling for life in the cool shade of their mightier ancestors. However, there was a gap in the leafy canopy overhead, just above the water, and the sun was now high enough to shine directly down on our pool, filling it with glittering flashes of light. The grass at the side of the stream was soft and mossy, warm and inviting. We walked the horses into the stream to cool their legs, and then left them loose to graze nearby. They seemed quite content not to roam, perhaps affected by the sense of peace that seemed to pervade this glade.

'We undressed, I still feeling slightly ill-at-ease at the exposure of the harsh light, and at the unusual feel of the air on my bare skin. Ryan had no such qualms and he jumped straight into the whirling pool. I followed a little more cautiously, somewhat concerned at being overlooked, although the place was so remote that it was in truth unlikely. But I had been brought up to be modest, and Ryan had to coax me, out of the cloak I had wrapped around my bare body, and into the water.

'Once I was in, however, I was taken by the heady delight of the water lashing against my skin, invading every corner of my body with cool, gentle fingers as we laughed and splashed. After a while though, the chill began to seep in, and we had to get out, shivering, onto the bank. We wrapped ourselves in the cloaks, and sat close together this way while we ate our food. We began to feel warmer and lay down, tangled together like puppies.

'After a while I became drowsy following the long ride, and I fell asleep. I dreamed that I awoke to find Ryan gone, and I sprang from sleep with a cry on my lips. Ryan was indeed gone from my side. I looked around frantically, and there he was, standing naked atop a large rock where it jutted from the water. I gasped, both at his temerity and at the wonderful sight he made. He did not hear me at first above the sound of the stream, and I was able to sit and observe him secretly for a while.

'I had discovered that it was considered entirely improper for a lady to admire the body of a man. I had found this out quite innocently a few days after the consummation of our marriage when being advised by the older married women. They had been shocked numb by my comments of how I loved Ryan to lie with me. They were totally horror-stricken when I asked, did they not find their husbands' parts delightful? So I took quiet, sinful pleasure now in imagining their faces if they could know what I was thinking at that moment. I called out to Ryan, overcome with desire, and wanting him to come to me.

'He jumped from rock to rock, quite unconscious of the spectacle he was creating, and ran to me where I sat. I tried to draw him down to me, but instead he remained standing, pulled off my cloak, and pushed me prone. Then he stood astride my naked body. He lowered himself, pushing his knees between mine, and he began to stroke my secret places softly, over and over, until I could barely stand it. I wondered with a gentle smile what the ladies of the house would think if they could see us now, totally, unashamedly, enjoying the sight and touch of each other. As always, when he finally entered me, I was more than ready for him. I knew this liberation of mine was entirely due to the gentle and patient handling Ryan had shown me on our wedding night. No bed-warmers and lonely nights for me, not like the other ladies seemed to prefer.

'This was one of the few times when Ryan showed any arrogance. He was totally confident in his ability to pleasure me, and he was right. God, how I adore him. But there is so much more to him than this. I had been warned that men had only one real need - to satisfy themselves at a woman's expense, treating her like a mere chattel, but Ryan does not behave that way. We talk for hours some nights, and he treats my every thought with respect.

'We did not leave the glade until it was almost too late to get home before dark, such was the hold it had on us.'

❦

Whilst it is extremely pleasant to relive such wonderful memories, it doesn't really help me come to terms with the past. It only makes my longing to see Ryan again with my own eyes even stronger. And I'm afraid there must be further rough waters ahead. Tony as ever is totally understanding of it all. Even these very intimate memories don't seem to trouble him. He knows that the body of Madeleine is no more my body now than the body of Garth is Ryan's. We are different physical people now. And, although he knows that I can recall Madeleine's feelings only too well sometimes, these events are in fact a long way in the past. Why has Tony been so understanding? I have to admit it puzzled me. It was only now, when I questioned him on it, that he explained why. When we were in the hypnotist's, she and I were upstairs, and Tony was downstairs - alone, except for a litter of puppies in a basket. Tony explained that he could hear some of what was going on upstairs. For instance he could hear me laughing at one point.

But it was when he heard me crying that the strangeness occurred which made him totally convinced of the truth of my whole experience. Obviously when he heard me so upset, his instinct was to come upstairs and see what was happening. But just as he was thinking of doing so, he noticed that the room temperature suddenly dropped about ten degrees. At the same moment the litter of puppies, that had been whimpering and crying, went dead quiet. Tony was sitting on a sofa with his back to the only door in the room. This door led into the hall of the house. He said he distinctly heard the door open behind him, and felt a presence come in and stand behind him. He said that, at that moment, nothing on earth would have persuaded him to turn round and see who it was. He heard a voice speak to him in a language he couldn't understand - but he understood the meaning. This being, whom I believe was the same spirit-guide that was steering my path upstairs, told him not to worry; that he must not go upstairs, and that the correct path was being followed up there. Then the door closed and the room temperature returned to normal.

This personal experience naturally had a great effect on his belief in the whole thing, and therefore, knowing that my experiences were real, that Ryan was real, he had no alternative but to accept it. He did of course, you may say, have another choice. He could have 'run a mile' - left me. But we are soul-mates, and so that was not an option. You can come to dislike a soul-mate if the circumstances dictate it, but you can never stop loving that person.

When I asked Tony why he had not told me of this before he said that he hadn't wanted to confuse me by muddying my waters with his own experiences. This showed me yet again how very lucky I am to have Tony. It demonstrates once more, I think, the difference between a 'normal' partner - and surface love, and the love of a soul-mate. I am, though, learning a lot about my hang-ups in my current lifetime from this past one. I think everybody who undergoes regression therapy does. For instance, I have always had a terrible dread of losing Tony in some way. Whenever he has to go away on business I over-react to the extreme, am afraid I may never see him again. Having these memories revealed explains such a lot. Obviously my life as Madeleine taught me that our lives can be ruined in a split second, and that we rarely have the control we think we have. Although I still do feel that fear I am more able to overcome it.

Back into 1996: our holiday plans were going ahead. We had actually paid for the flight (three planes in one day! What a baptism of fire!). And Tony still couldn't believe how far I had come - from being totally, unequivocally opposed to any kind of air travel to volunteering for this! I had seen him give me the odd incredulous glance as we sat signing the necessary papers for our journey.

I tried to plan a way to meet Garth while we were out there. I was willing to try almost anything to meet or, at least, see him - anything that wouldn't damage my relationship with Tony, and anything that wouldn't offend Garth or risk his disapproval or upset his wife, of course. I didn't even know if he would be in Nashville at the same time as us, but we would be staying in Goodlettsville, and, I had a very strong feeling, not far from where he lived. So, if he was home, and if the fates allowed it, we might see him there. I also wrote to his management offices, asking if there was any way at all that we could see him in Nashville. I hoped that the fact that we were coming all the way from England, and that it would be the first time I had found the courage to fly (I hoped!), might encourage them to help us. I knew the odds were stacked against us, but I had no intention of letting that spoil this holiday of a lifetime. I was very excited at the prospect of seeing some of America, a place that had always held a fascination for me.

I felt that I would get on very well with the American people as I loved their general enthusiasm. I also loved the idea of a big country, some of its parts not yet even tamed by invasive man. I have always been fiercely patriotic of my English roots but finally my eyes had been opened to that great big world out there. They had been opened by seeing Garth, and not only as a result of our past-life connection but also by his obvious zest for life. A little of it had rubbed off. He'd awakened the explorer in me. I had always been afraid of change, but now I realised sometimes change is good.

Another happy memory I have had from Madeleine was of an event that took place every year on a day in September. It was the annual apple harvesting day. This was the day when all the apples were picked and made into cider. As Madeleine I shared three such days with Ryan. I only wish it had been more. Here is her memory of one such day.

'The leaves on the apple trees in the orchard were just starting to lose their vitality. Their edges were dry and curling, gradually changing from green to brown. By contrast, the apples themselves shone with life, rosy and vibrant, all the energy of the tree locked inside them. Some had fallen, though, and lay chewed, open, half-eaten by wasps and birds, their sweet juices sucked from them.

'Apple harvesting was always a happy time. Everyone (except Mother and Father of course), joined in the task. Two ponies stood patiently in the shade, waiting for their carts to be filled with fruit. Every little while I would fetch the ponies an apple as a reward. Laughter filled the air for this was easy work compared with the men's usual labours. Whole families toiled happily together, camaraderie strongly in evidence, everyone anticipating the taste of the cider. And, back in the dairy, preparations were under way for the pressing of the cider. Ryan and I were together, and that was all we ever needed. Being by far the taller of the two of us, Ryan plucked the apples and handed them down to me to be placed in a wicker basket. When the basket was full, he would carry it to one of the carts.

'At midday, servants brought a picnic luncheon to the orchard for everyone, the workers' payment for the day. There was no difference on this day between the workers and those high-born among us, and I think that this was one of the reasons why Ryan loved it so. I knew he also loved the sense of belonging to one big family. I never saw him laugh so much as he did on these occasions, and I treasured such days dearly. Everyone sat on the grass to eat, leaning on the trees, and on each other. Ryan sat down, resting his back against one of the old gnarled trunks, and I lay outstretched with my head on his lap. Sighing deeply, he linked his hands behind his head and closed his eyes, an expression of sheer bliss on his face.

'Later in the afternoon when the picking was done, when the trees stood bare of their splendid treasure, when the apples were all back at the dairy being pressed in readiness for the fermentation into that delicious and powerful drink, games were organised. The children's favourite game was apple-bobbing. Tubs of water had apples floating in them, and the contestants had to keep their hands behind their backs while leaning forwards, trying to snatch an apple, and using only their mouths and teeth. Naturally the apples were pushed beneath the water during these attempts and everyone got wonderfully wet trying to capture these elusive trophies. Several of the children, giggling and egging each other on, and knowing that he would be a willing victim, approached Ryan. They grasped his hands and arms and pulled him; he struggling in mock protest. Once beside the bobbing apples, he entered fully into the spirit of things, plunging his head beneath the water. The trick, as he knew, was to push an apple right to the bottom of the tub, heedless of the water, and grip it against the bottom with your teeth. He was greeted with gleeful shrieks from the children when he reared up from the tub, an apple clenched in his teeth, his hair soaking wet, spraying water droplets over them as he deliberately shook his head. He came back to me, presented me with his apple, and smiling, hugged me to him, thereby effectively soaking me too with his streaming wet hair and his equally wet shirt front. This performance was watched by the children with much amusement. He looked so happy. His eyes were aglow with laughter, his hair plastered to his head, and his life-force was bubbling so incandescently that I hugged the moment to myself to savour it in the future.

'Then the children wanted to venture into the woods to play "hide and go seek", and, of course, nothing would do except that Ryan play too. He agreed happily, and he and the children, all but one who was to "seek", ran into the trees to hide. I was to help the seeker, and so after counting to the obligatory one hundred, we set off to find the others. Those in hiding had to try and make their way, behind our backs, to "home", the orchard, before we could "tag" them.

'A lot of the children sneaked past us and made it home, but most of the others we chased and tagged. Soon, only one boy, and Ryan, remained unfound. The tagged children joined us in the hunt, but all the hollow trees and other convenient hiding places had already been searched to no avail. A group of us was passing beneath an ancient oak when all was revealed. Suddenly, so that we were startled, Ryan dropped into sight, dangling upside down from the large branch he had climbed up to, and where he had been hidden from us by the foliage. He had his legs hooked over the branch, and

56

thus he was suspended, his hair loose and trailing towards the ground. In his arms he held the missing boy, who now dropped gleefully to the ground, and, taking advantage of our surprise, he made off and ran home to the orchard. Ryan however could not escape us. Willing hands reached for him as the children jumped up, grasping his arms, and soon, by the sheer weight of the number clinging to him, he was pulled from the tree. He landed sprawled on the ground, hidden momentarily by the squealing children as they swarmed triumphantly over him. I stood back while the excited young ones scrambled to their feet and pulled Ryan up too. Then I followed behind as they dragged their prize captive back to the orchard.

'As twilight descended, our picnic supper arrived, and, united in the satisfaction of hard work, and hard play, we sat together around a bonfire and ate this modest feast.

'We did not retire to bed until after midnight this day, and as I drifted to sleep, I could not help but thank God for days such as this one. Days like this sustained us and gave us strength to face tougher times.'

Chapter Six

Today, in 1996, a friend has said that perhaps this tale should not be published, as it is too personal. The way I felt at first I should have agreed. However, now I think that I owe it to Ryan to bring him to light. He had a short life and a tragic end which was never recorded. He was such a truly unique and special person (for even Garth is no longer really Ryan, and so Ryan, as he was, no longer exists) that it is a crime that he had little opportunity in that life to give the world what he had to offer; I feel great bitterness at times that the world never mourned his passing.

In those days of little compassion or respect for life, he was very unusual with his caring and gentle nature. I also feel that I owe it to Madeleine who suffered a terrible injustice, and lived the rest of her life in lonely suffering. It makes me cry still, whenever I feel her despair and helplessness. And although her parents can never be brought to justice, at least the record can be set straight.

Ryan was the only man Madeleine ever saw cry. It was not the done thing for a man to show his emotions that way. This is how it happened.

'I came upon him one day, holding a tiny fox cub as it breathed its last. He cradled the small creature in his hands as if willing it to live, but it could not. I realised with real surprise that he had tears on his cheeks. My first thought was to make away to save him any shame, but in truth I was delighted to discover his genuine care for a fellow creature, no matter how lowly. To my further surprise, when he saw me there he did not try to wipe the tears or hide them. He gently placed the dead cub on the ground, and then pulled me close for comfort. As I held him tightly, I could see that the cub's mother lay bloody on the ground at Ryan's feet. He told me that he had come across two men tormenting the vixen. They had her in a trap and were poking at her with sticks. When Ryan had shouted at them to stop they had stabbed her with the sticks so that she died.

'What had so upset Ryan was that minutes later, when the men had gone, the cub had crawled out of the undergrowth, and lay down crying at its mother's side. The cub was sickly and half-starved, and had died as I had seen. I think the tears may have had something to do with the memory of his own mother.' [Perhaps, had Ryan and Madeleine been allowed to live out their natural span together, she may have been able to draw some of this poison from his mind. But at the time all she could offer was the comfort of her arms.]

In the early days of their marriage Ryan and Madeleine faced some unexpected challenges. This was entirely due to her parents' stubborn refusal to give the marriage credence by making it public knowledge. There follows the accounts of two such incidents.

July 1638 (three months after the wedding)

'Ryan was busy digging over the beds of the kitchen garden late one afternoon when Mother passed through accompanied by Evelyn Wells, an influential lady of the county who was at that time a house guest. She was a very beautiful lady with red hair and green eyes.

'At the moment that they were passing Ryan was crouched down, prising a large stone out of the soil with his hands so that he could continue digging. Evelyn paused at the end of this vegetable bed, and Ryan glanced sidelong up at them. [This is a look special to both Ryan and Garth. There is something about the eyes that capture your heart when they look at you this way.] Evelyn had never seen Ryan before, and she seemed intrigued.

'She laid a hand on my mother's arm to delay her, and asked her quietly, "Who is this young man, Margaret?"

'"He is no-one," Mother replied firmly, her eyes daring Ryan to correct her. "He is merely one of the servants."

'Ryan turned his gaze from Evelyn to Mother, and smiled, her discomfiture amusing him somewhat. Then he stood up, and forcefully slamming the spade deep into the earth, he continued turning the soil over, the soft smile never leaving his face. Evelyn made no move to continue walking, but stood staring at Ryan as he worked.

'A predatory look came into her eyes, and she said, "I have need of a new worker. I should like to

60

employ him." She called out to Ryan, "You there, what is your name?"

'Before he could reply, Mother took hold of Evelyn's arm and hurriedly drew her on towards the house, saying, "I am sorry, Evelyn, but he cannot be spared from here. We are short-handed at present."

'She could answer no other way for obviously Ryan would not have agreed to such a change of employment. Mother did not want him to reveal the truth of his position, and he might do so were he pressured by Evelyn. Some time later, Mother reappeared at Ryan's side, alone this time. She commanded of him, "If Evelyn speaks to you again, you are not to answer. Do you understand me?"

'Ryan turned to face her and stuck the spade into the ground. He braced one foot on the top edge of the blade and leaned his arms on the handle.

'Then he answered, "If she speaks to me, I must answer. You would not want your servants to gain a reputation for dumb insolence - would you?"

'" Well - do not attempt to enhance your position in her eyes."

'"You mean, do not tell her that I am your daughter's husband?" he asked with a totally innocent look, eyebrows raised.

'"Yes!" she hissed.

'Ryan smiled at her once more and said, "Very well, it is of no importance to me that you deny me as your son-in-law. I will allow you your pride, foolish though it is."

'Pursing her lips in irritation, despite his promise, Mother went back to the house, passing me on the way as I came to fetch Ryan for his supper.

'She spat at me in passing, "Your fortune hunter does not even make a good servant!"

61

'However she had left Ryan in a difficult position that even she did not anticipate, for it appeared that Evelyn had been greatly attracted to him, and she was not a lady to be easily denied. She presumed him to be unmarried, and, as a servant, available to her in any way that she desired.

'So, two hours later, when Ryan was in the loft of the big barn, stacking hay, Evelyn came to him. She hitched up her skirts in a most unladylike manner, then climbed the ladder up to him.

'Ryan continued to work, but as a servant would do, he asked her, "Can I help you, my Lady?"

'"Yes, I believe you can," she replied, stepping up close to him, and laying her hand on the pitchfork so that he was forced to stop work. "What is your name?"

'"Ryan," he replied.

'"Well - Ryan - there is a service I require of you. A service I am sure you will enjoy. Come with me at once to my bedchamber." She met his eyes unashamedly, her own green eyes gleaming as she left him in no doubt as to her requirements of him.

'"I am sorry, my Lady, I cannot," he replied, folding his arms across his chest in a defensive gesture. "In any case, I would not be permitted in that part of the house."

'She placed a hand softly on each of his forearms, saying, "The place does not matter." Now her eyes grew soft and her lashes lowered. "This place will suffice as well as anywhere. It is warm and comfortable," she purred, eyeing the soft piles of hay, "There is no-one to see us."

'Ryan dropped his hands to his sides, so that her hands fell from him. "I am sorry, I cannot." he repeated. "I have a great deal of work to complete before dark."

'She stepped even closer, her breasts brushing against him, and she looked up at him, her eyes hungry now, her lips slightly parted.

'After a pause she replied, "You misunderstand me, this is not a request; it is an order." She put her arms around his neck, stretched up on her toes and lifted her mouth to his. But he drew his head back out of reach, and gently took hold of her wrists, pulling her arms from his neck.

'"I am married," he pointed out, showing her the ring on his finger.

'"That is no concern of mine," she responded, sounding a little angry now. Then her tone softened, "Listen, I too am married, but my husband is an infertile man. I must have a child. Time is running out for me..." She paused, "...your eyes are such a remarkable colour. I would love to have a child with your eyes. I do not require your future or your allegiance, only your seed. I am told I am beautiful, and no doubt you are married to some fat peasant, so how can you refuse me? Come—" she tried to lead him deeper into the lengthening shadows, but he resisted her.

'"You truly are a beautiful woman, but my wife is equally beautiful, and I love her. We have taken and given a vow which will never be broken. Please - I ask you to respect this."

'She was a little taken aback at this declaration, and she said, "Even if I tell you that I will make certain you lose your position here?"

'"Yes."

'"Even if I swear that your wife would never know?"

'"Yes."

'"Then this peasant wife of yours is very fortunate, and I hope she understands her good fortune—" She left the sentence hanging, and a little wistfully trailed a finger-tip down Ryan's chest, before she turned and left the barn.

'Later when Ryan and I were alone together, I could sense that he had something to tell me. He stepped up close and rested his arms lightly on my shoulders, lacing his fingers together loosely at the nape of my neck. Our eyes were inches apart, blue on blue. I could see that he was greatly troubled, for although he was trying to project a lightness of spirit, his eyes could never lie to me.

'"What is it my love?" I prompted.

'"Something happened this afternoon..." he hesitated, "...well in fact nothing really happened...but I am concerned that word might get back to you, either through Evelyn, for she does not know that you are my wife, or from another more malicious source...if she finds out from Evelyn."

'"You mean my mother?"

'"Yes, Madeleine, I do."

'"She could say nothing bad about you that I would believe. You know this has been attempted before."

'"But this time Evelyn may - they may conspire together to convince you—" His voice petered out, and he unlaced his hands, cupping my face in them tenderly, his eyes intense.

'"Ryan, what has happened? You must tell me yourself, so that there is no misunderstanding."

'His eyes dropped; he was obviously embarrassed, and he spoke with downcast eyes.

'"It would seem that she had chosen me to father her a child." His eyes lifted searchingly to mine once more, anxious to gauge my reaction to this revelation.

'"So what happened?" I asked, shocked.

'"Nothing happened; I refused her. You must know I would never—"

'"But what happened? Tell me!" I insisted.

'"Very well, very well." Ryan raised his hands placatingly, thinking that I was close to anger now. He obviously did not relish telling me the details, but he knew I would not be denied.

'He began. "Evelyn came to me when I was alone in the loft over the barn, and asked - no, demanded that I lie with her."

'"And?" I asked quietly.

'"Madeleine!" he exclaimed, shocked in turn. "You must know that I would never betray you."

'I laid my hands against his chest and smiled up at his worried face because the truth was written plain in his expression. He let out a long sigh of relief and hugged me to him, my hands now captive between us.

'Then he continued his tale. "She told me, when I refused her, that she would tell your mother, in order that I would be dismissed, and I was afraid that your mother would then come to you with a lie."

'"How did she try to tempt you?" I asked, still curious, and I confess, though I was hiding it desperately, a little concerned as to what exactly had happened. I believed that Ryan had not bedded Evelyn but I was feeling a growing sense of indignation at the thought of what my imagination was showing me. Best I knew the truth of it.

'Eventually I drew it out of him - all of it, the touching, the attempted kiss, the soft persuasive words, and the threats and promises. By then I was truly indignant. How dare she lay hands on him! I had never felt this way before. So this was jealousy. I did not like this feeling. I wanted to seek Evelyn out and confront her as Ryan's wife. But I knew this would cause him a great deal more trouble because of his promise to Mother.

'Ryan must have felt the tension in my body, for once more his hands found my face, and he lifted my chin so that our eyes met. "It was nothing," he soothed, one hand reaching up to stroke my hair. "Nothing would ever tempt me. I will always be only yours." He could see, though, that I was still angry at Evelyn, so he continued, "When I found you I found everything I have ever wanted. I will never hurt you, and I would not risk the horror of losing you just for the sake of a brief moment of pleasure. And when it comes to you, only you—I would stop at nothing to make you happy. No one else will ever matter to me."

'His eyes embraced mine, and I knew that he spoke the truth. But still this new feeling would not be shaken off lightly. Jealousy, I discovered, was a very ugly emotion. I still felt very angry with Evelyn. It was true she did not know that she had wronged me for she did not know that Ryan was my husband. But now I also began to see why Ryan had such disdain for the majority of rich folk. Because it would, I realised, have been just as bad for me had I been the fat peasant she supposed me to be. Yet she thought this disregard for Ryan's wife to be acceptable, just because she, Evelyn, thought her to be a mere peasant. She would be mortified, no doubt, if she discovered the truth. Once more I was tempted to confront her with this truth.

'But now I became distracted, for Ryan's touch had become a caress, and delicious shivers were commanding my attention. I capitulated to him with a contented sigh, for he was - after all - mine.

'This kind of misunderstanding had occurred on other occasions, due entirely to Mother's stubborn refusal to acknowledge our marriage. I had some difficulty with a previous suitor of mine. His name was Robert Simmonds and he was a pleasant enough young man, but he had never held any real interest for me. He came to visit unexpectedly, two weeks after our wedding, and apparently was with Mother and Father for over an hour before he sought me out. I had walked down to the bridge over the stream to await Ryan's return from the furthest fields of the estate, and I was sitting on the narrow parapet watching for him when Robert appeared. As he joined me, my first thought was that I must tell him immediately of my marriage, but before I could do so, after only a brief and nervous greeting, he got straight down on one knee, and I realised with horror that his intention was to propose to me. He took my hand while I was still trying to find the right words. But before he could begin to speak, his attention was drawn sharply to something off to one side of the bridge.

'I turned to look, and there stood Ryan. He had his arms crossed over his chest, and, with his brows raised and a slight smile on his lips, he waited there with apparent interest to see what was to happen.

'"Madeleine," Robert asked, "who is this?"

'I held up my hand to forestall him from speaking further, "Robert I am sorry to disappoint you, but this is my husband, Ryan Fitzgerald."

'I had always thought of Robert as a level-headed person, and he had never given me cause to think otherwise, but at this information, he suddenly sprang to his feet, and unexpected menace poured from him in tangible waves. "Your husband!" he shouted, "This commoner! I do not believe it! Do you try to make a fool of me?"

'"I am sorry—" I began, but he interrupted me.

'"Nobody will make a fool of me, else they live to regret it!"

'Then he grasped my wrist and pulled me to my feet, and close to him.

'Ryan, quite serious now, stepped forward, and taking hold of my shoulders from behind, turned me aside, out of harm's way.

'Then he stood between us, "I am Madeleine's husband," he stated with quiet authority.

'"No!" Robert denied this. Then he took hold of Ryan's shirt with both hands and shoved him roughly. In response, Ryan thrust his arms between Robert's and took hold of his shirt too, shoving him backwards with equal force. They continued this way, for unusually here was someone who matched Ryan in height and weight, and they pushed each other back and forth across the narrow bridge. Then Ryan, with a grunt of effort, forced Robert backwards until he crashed into the bridge's guard-rail, which creaked alarmingly, till I was certain it would break, and both men would plummet down into the stream, twenty feet below. But in the end it was only Robert who fell. He swung a wild punch at Ryan just as the rail snapped, and this unbalanced him, so that he tumbled into space. He did however, manage to arrest his fall, by catching hold of the edge of the bridge. He would have soon fallen though, had Ryan not grasped his arm, and held him fast until he could climb back to safety. Even once he was safe, Robert leapt to his feet, and once more stood eye to eye with Ryan, unable to back down.

'I felt sorry for Robert. His pride had been hurt, that was all. He must have gained my parents' permission to ask for my hand - no wonder he had not believed me. Why in the name of God had they not told him? - to cause mischief obviously. I was determined they would not succeed, so I squeezed between the two of them, and looked Robert in the eye.

'"I am sorry," I said once again. "Our marriage has caused great discord in the family, so it has not been made public knowledge. No-one meant to demean you, please—" With a snarl on his lips, Robert turned and strode from the grounds. I never saw him again.'

Tony and I often contemplate in wonder the many and varied ways Garth has affected our lives without him even knowing about it. It really is as if someone has thrown a pebble in a pond, and the ever-widening ripples are still spreading out. Not long after seeing that first TV concert, and after I had started song-writing, Tony decided he would like a hat the same as Garth's - a Stetson. I had always had a hankering for one because I do suffer from sunstroke in the summertime. So we tracked down a Western clothes shop. We bought a hat each and while we were there I couldn't help but admire the magnificent Western saddles. I'd had horses for years and though I had often admired Western gear, I had never tried it. The owners of the shop kindly offered to let me try one of their fully trained quarter horses. As soon as I mounted the horse I knew this style of riding was for me. I sold my horse-box, and I bought a small car and the complete set of Western tack. I then went about changing twenty years of English riding experience and began to re-train my older horse to Western style.

As if these changes to our lifestyle weren't enough, once I had some completed songs, I hired a session singer to record them onto a demo tape for me. Following on from that, Tony and I went to see his country band play, and while we were there became very impressed with Western line dancing. Eventually we started going to lessons, and we still go to this day. So you can see that Garth has had a tremendous impact on our lives in every way. We feel our lives are enhanced by this contact with him. It's at times like this I contemplate with almost awe what kind of an effect could we expect if we ever made personal contact. Then I feel a little sad, and wonder if we'll ever get the chance to find out. It seems terribly cruel of fate to let me rediscover 'Ryan', only to deny me any access to him in this lifetime.

Today I have had some new and terrible memories from Madeleine. They have left me shocked once more at the intensity of her love for Ryan. It also helped to explain to me the inevitable intensity of my feelings for a man I have never met in this lifetime.

June 1640 (almost three weeks after Ryan was kidnapped)

'I know now that Ryan will never come back to me. It tears my heart in two even to think of it, but I have such a terrible feeling. Last night there was a summer storm, and it filled me with dread such as I have never known. I have never been afraid of storms before, but last night as I tried to sleep on the rugs in front of the fire (for I can no longer bear to lay alone in our bed), the wind seemed to be trying to

70

tear the house apart. The chimney groaned like some giant beast. The storm seemed to me like a harbinger of doom.

'I was sure he (Ryan) lay somewhere in the dark, wet, cold, and alone - my arms ached to hold him - my hands to touch him - my whole body yearned to lie against him - but I never will again...

'This morning the colour has leached out of my world and everything is total desolation.

'I went for a ride on Ryan's favourite horse, Cherish, and galloped wildly and recklessly through the woods. Branches lashed at us in the wind, and sent Cherish into a frenzy of speed. When we came to the meadow, our meadow, I reined her in - Oh God, I cannot bear this feeling - I pleaded with the wind to take my spirit away and spread it into the sky, then maybe I would not have to feel anything any more.

'Uselessly I cried out loud "Ryan!—Ryan!" over and over, praying, begging, that somehow he would hear me and come back to me. But the wind snatched my voice away, and I was still there alone...Tears are no longer enough. I do not think I can go on. This relentless pain is destroying me. I feel as if a living part of me has been cruelly wrenched from my body and it will never, never heal.

'I rode Cherish back to the woods, at a walking pace now, my energy spent. When I reached the glade that holds our tree, I sat for a moment staring at the late bluebells that still survived in the shady depths. A wave of fresh torment battered me, and I threw myself from the horse's back. I fell to the ground; grief, fear, and frustration bringing me to my knees. I knelt amid the faded blooms and closed my eyes. My mind tried to bring me comfort by drawing me back into the precious past. All around

71

me there appeared a sea of newly sprung bluebells. And Ryan walking towards me, a smile on his face. He loved the bluebells so; their ability to produce such an extravagant profusion of blossoms was a joyous celebration of life to him. They were rampant and unstoppable, flowing like blue fire under the trees. As he came nearer, I was struck by the way his eyes reflected the blue power that was spread at his feet.

'I was transported for a while, but inevitably the dream dissolved, and I opened my eyes on a world that I had nothing but loathing for. A sob caught in my throat as I realised with horror that if I were to remain in this world, then next spring I would have to endure the bluebells alone. It would be unbearable - how could they still live if he did not?

⚜

'How could they do it(my parents)? I will never understand. Sometimes in the house I fly into a sudden rage. Nothing and no-one is safe from me. The servants hide from me at these times. They are right to be afraid of me.

'Ryan would not like me this way. He would not like my grief to change me so much. But I fear that this Madeleine is here to stay. The old me has died long since. I am not permitted even to wear widows' weeds, as they, (my parents) are trying to deny that we were ever wed…I grow so angry now. Ryan was snatched from this world that he could have given so much to. I have lost everything I ever wanted while they continue as if nothing has happened.

'Ryan was always so much stronger than I. At times like this I remember when he showed that strength of character and try to draw help from it. One such time was when she (my mother) decided Ryan was not doing enough to earn our keep. She had been taunting him about it, so that when he was given a task to complete one day in July (1639), his stubborn Irish pride would not let him stop until it was finished. He was told to dig a pit in the grounds of the house. It was to be a large pit, too much for one man to dig in a day. But that was the demand.

'It was dark by the time he came in to our bedchamber, so stiff and tired that he could barely walk. He spoke not a word, but fell into the chair, and then rested his arms on the table, and lowered his head to lean it on them. I stood behind him not knowing how to help. When I touched his arms I could feel the muscles there trembling with fatigue. Ryan had taught me how to rub him with oils to help his muscles relax, so he undressed and lay in front of the fire, the flames flickering like candlelight over his naked body. The rubbing motion soothed him and me, and soon the soothing turned to arousal.

'The next afternoon when we rode past the pit, it had been filled in, looking like a grave [Knowing what I know of Madeleine's mother I suspect this was no coincidence, but very symbolic, and if she could have made it Ryan's grave she would have done]. It was obvious to both of us that his labours had been nothing but a cruel trick. Ryan did not say a word, but I could tell how angry he was by the way his jaw line tightened, and the way his hands clenched on the reins.'

Chapter Seven

I have been shown the first time Madeleine really became aware of just how deep and dangerous her mother's hatred of Ryan was becoming. It frightened her but, sadly, not enough to make her leave her father who had become ill. Had she but known how her father was to betray them both, she would have wished him to die and release her. Maybe then her dearest Ryan would not have died.

It was also at this point that I had the sudden realisation that Margaret was actually Madeleine's stepmother, not her natural mother.

June 1638

'On this day we had gone for one of our long rides. We were deep in the forest, having taken a wrong path, and the horses had grown very nervous. Suddenly a wild boar crashed through the undergrowth, and both horses took flight. Perhaps Ryan could have stopped his horse's bolt but I could not stop mine. I began a terrifying headlong gallop, dangerous to both my limbs and the mare's. I could hear Ryan's horse close behind.

'Eventually, inevitably, my horse crashed down. I narrowly avoided her flailing hooves as she struggled back to her feet and then made off. Ryan's horse flew past me at great speed. Uncharacteristically, Ryan I think, panicked. After he had managed to bring his mare to a halt, instead of holding her firmly, he dismounted and let her go. His only thought seemed to be to run back to me to see if I were hurt. I cried out a warning but it was too late. The mare took to her heels after her companion. As Ryan and I stared at each other in dismay, the sound of their flight receded into the far distance, and silence descended on the forest. Only after a few long moments did the normal background noise of the woodlands return. I was unhurt, and Ryan looked at me, his blue eyes wide and slightly chastened by his mistake. I smiled, and he smiled ruefully back.

'We did not know quite what we were to do. We did not know where we were. It was cloudy and there was no sun to guide us. Ryan was clever but he was not a woodsman. We had been travelling steadily for two hours before we lost our way, and after our headlong dash we could be anywhere. Of course the horses, as horses do, once they had outrun their fear, would unerringly find their way home. Then the alarm would be raised but how would they know where to look?

'For a while we struggled through the undergrowth, looking for a path, disturbing the animals with our noise. Eventually we found a track but we were not sure of which way to turn. We chose what we hoped was the correct direction, and walked, still cheerful, hand in hand, listening to the bird song, revelling in the signs of late spring and our quiet companionship. Bluebells formed a magic carpet in each clearing. In places they were so dense that the very air was tinged with blue. But gradually we grew concerned as the light grew dimmer, yet neither of us wanting to admit the fact to the other. We came to a fork, and in silent agreement, took the instinctual course to the left. It was wrong as after a while the path began to peter out. Rather than retrace our steps, Ryan made his second mistake, and decided that we should take the shorter route through the trees. We got hopelessly lost again, turned again, and were mystified. It began to rain. Ryan was mortified. His face looked so contrite, I likened him to a whipped puppy, and I could not help but laugh at him. After a while he joined me in laughter. But our laughter was short-lived. The rain grew heavier, falling now in plump pearls of water that soaked us in seconds.

'We were becoming cold. I began to recall tales of robbers and brigands who were said to prowl these forests at night, preying on those unwise enough to venture there after dark. But at least I had Ryan to watch over me while he carried the burden of safekeeping for both of us. We found a hollow tree trunk and huddled together inside it to share the warmth of our bodies. It was becoming too dark to see our way, and we knew that in parts of the forest there were deep and treacherous pits. And, by now, we had no idea if we were near them.

'What we could not know, was that one of our poor horses, Fallow, had slipped and fallen into one of those very pits. The men sent to find us after Cherish had raised the alarm followed her trail back through the undergrowth, and found the marks that Fallow's hooves had made on the stones as she frantically tried to halt her downward plunge. One of our bags was on the ground nearby where it had become dislodged from her saddle. There were no sounds from below, and it was too dark to see into the bottom of the pit so the worst was feared - that one or both of us had plunged to our deaths and lay at the bottom.

'The stars came out and thus we were able to discover which direction to make for. We stayed in the hollow tree until early light, and then set off for home. As it happened, we were nearer than we had realised, and two hours later we arrived safely home.

'The revelation came to me concerning Mother as we were going through the gardens. She only saw me at first because Ryan had gone to the stables to check on the horses. She showed what seemed to be genuine motherly concern, as much as she had ever done.

'Placing her hands on my shoulders and smiling, she said, "Madeleine my child, I feared you killed."

'At that moment Ryan appeared around the corner of the buildings. With her face directly in front of my eyes there was no concealing her immediate reaction. Her mouth twisted into a grimace of distaste and she glared at him malevolently. I realised later that her smile had indeed been one of gratitude but not for my safe return - because on seeing me, she had presumed that Ryan had been the one tossed into the pit with Fallow. She turned without a word and stalked into the house. It came to me with horror that she did not just hate him, she actually wished to see him dead.'

1996

A few rather disjointed thoughts have crossed my mind which I will tell you here. I feel Madeleine is about to reveal something dreadful to me and my own thoughts are jumping squirrel-like in anticipation.

Tony has reminded me that I have always shown a fascination for old portraits, and always from around the 1600s. I have often stood trying to see the person in the portrait as a real three-dimensional character, and usually succeeded. How very strange it will be, if I ever come across a portrait of Madeleine. Sadly I know I will never find one of Ryan, because of his poor background.

A small comforting thought occurred to me last night as I looked up at the stars. And that was that allowing for universal shifts over the centuries, Madeleine, Ryan, Garth, Sandy, and Tony and I have all shared those same stars, even when we were apart. It brings us all closer somehow.

I feel that it is possible that Ryan died in sight of Lumley Castle near Sunderland. I will be able to confirm this if I can find a picture of the castle one day.

⚜

The memory I didn't want to see has come.

This is the hardest part of Madeleine's story I have had to write. She showed it to me last night. Tony had gone to bed and I had fallen into a light sleep on the sofa. She woke me a little after midnight. I had a feeling this was coming but it was still a shock.

August Thirty-first 1640 (about three months after Ryan's abduction)

'I think madness has finally overtaken me. I drift like a wraith through a fantasy world. People talk to me but I do not hear them - they speak to me as though through a mist. I talk to Ryan at night and sometimes I even hear him answer me. Days ago I found some of his hair entwined in my hairbrush, though I swear it was not there before. I have woven it into a ring and I wear it all the time. Now when I walk in the woods I often see Ryan. He is always shadowy, partly hidden, and just out of reach. I try to follow him. Sometimes I even see him here in the house...

'I see him now. He is climbing the stairs, and I follow him...he is going up into the attic, and I follow him...I can see him through the window, on the roof and I climb out of the window to him...I cannot see him immediately but then I hear him calling my name. He is below, in the courtyard, holding up his arms to me. I trust him completely so, with no fear at all, I step off the roof. Seemingly in slow motion, I fly, down and down, into his waiting arms...Thank God.'

❧

I cried for a while after writing this. Finally I had to go and waken poor Tony so that he could comfort me. All I could think about Madeleine was: poor little thing. But eventually came a sense of relief. Her last thought on this earth had been, thank God, and I thanked him too. She was at peace.

The next day

I felt a huge sense of release today. The pressure that has been building since I began this regression has finally lifted somewhat. I don't feel quite so desperate. I wonder if maybe a small fragment of my spirit was still locked in that Elizabethan house, not free to progress until this awful injustice was revealed in its entirety, and that now it has joined me. It will be fascinating to discover if the house has had a reputation for being haunted. When Madeleine died everything went black. I did have a great sense of loss at her leaving me but I feel that the small part of her that remained in this world after her body left it is now at rest.

When I first saw Garth Brooks, I was filled with a sense of euphoria, but, as I began to realise that something was fighting to be heard, I began to feel more desperate than satisfied. I still want to meet him if I possibly can - it would mean so much to me. I long to look into Ryan's eyes once more because I still mourn him.

I have, however, come to realise that I have been made more complete, now that the remaining part of Madeleine's spirit has come to me. It's as if someone has given me extra confidence. Confidence is something I have always lacked in this lifetime. I feel adventurous. I see some things, like aeroplanes for instance, as if for the first time. And Madeleine, who had a much more courageous attitude to life, made me want to try a ride in one, instead of shying away from the danger, real or imaginary. When I walk down the street, I have a new bounce in my step, and my attitude is much more assertive. I have always had trouble saying no, whereas Madeleine did not, and several people have come to notice this difference in me, without knowing the reason why. As for my relationship with Tony, without going into details which are too personal, every aspect has been enhanced by the arrival of this new, mischievous, and more sensual side to my character.

She also loves Tony as much as I do - I suppose she was bound to, as I think I love Ryan as much as she did.

Chapter Eight

I feel so pleased! I was afraid that, with the revelation of her death, Madeleine's memories would no longer reach my conscious mind, but I was wrong. I believe now that I am to be shown the rest of Ryan and Madeleine's life together. For a start she has shown me a wrong assumption I made. I had assumed that there could be no portrait of Ryan because of his poor background. But this morning, just after I had woken up, I saw her clearly, sitting holding a portrait of him. It is quite small and looks to be in the cheaper medium of pastels rather than oils. I will advertise in some magazines to see if anyone has this portrait, or one of Madeleine.

I have mentioned my friend who is psychic. I first met her two years ago. I remember saying to everyone, including Tony, that it was very strange how I felt I had known her for years. Have you ever met anyone that had that effect on you? We have only met face to face three times, and yet I am able to discuss anything with her. When I began to investigate my past lives, and proved myself open to such things, she said, 'Of course you realise that we have known each other before?' As soon as she

81

had said it, it became so obvious to me. We are both at present making notes on our meditations, without consulting each other, to see if we can come up with any matching lifetimes.

It was at around this time that more odd things started to occur in our everyday life. I had been told that this would happen. It was another sign that my psychic abilities had been awoken, and were growing. I know a lot of people don't believe in this either, but again science helps to prove it. It is accepted that we have an area of our brain that doesn't seem to serve any useful purpose. No-one seems really to know what it is for. I believe this is where our psychic centre lies. And as for those who still doubt this I would respectfully point out that one hundred years ago, or less, if you had told someone that by now almost every person in the Western world would have a small box in their home; that people from hundreds, even thousands of miles away, would send pictures to them all; that they would do this by converting those pictures into tiny dots which would travel unseen through the air, sometimes bouncing off an artificial moon; that the small box would then translate this back into pictures, so that you could see, as it happened, an event on the other side of the world - they would, at worst, have burnt you for a witch, and, at best, called you the world's biggest fool. But today we all have one of these magic boxes, despite the fact that very few of us even understand how television works.

I have also had brief snatches of other lifetimes during self-hypnosis. But I think they have, until now, been overshadowed by the need to resolve the story of Ryan and Madeleine.

One such story involved Tony. I had vivid sight and sensation of being dragged along a hallway in a castle. It was very strange on two counts: first, I was a boy, and second, I was only about ten, and very small. It was totally weird to experience the feelings of being light enough to be manhandled in this way. It was like being hauled aloft by a giant. I remember cannoning into a wooden chair, and I have been able to sketch this chair. When we reached the great hall I was tossed onto a red carpet. I have no doubt that I was to have been killed, as I had apparently been found, not for the first time, stealing food from the kitchens. But a tall stranger stepped between myself and my would-be attacker. The bully was obviously intimidated by this stranger who I came to understand was Tony. It was plain that he was a Knight, although he was not dressed in armour at the time. He faced my assailant down, forcing him to back off, and announced that I would become his squire.

Sadly there is not much left to relate. The next scene was at a tournament, and, on entering my Knight's tent, I discovered him lying murdered. He had been stabbed twice in the back while he had lain with a lady. The lady had also been slain.

Strangely, the night after this memory, I had to awaken Tony from a violent nightmare. Tony does not usually have vivid dreams, and does not usually remember them anyway. But he was shouting in his sleep. When I managed to wake him, which was quite difficult, he said that he had been in bed with a lady - it was not me. On the wall he had seen what could have been a helmet and a jousting lance. The reason he had been shouting was that he was being attacked from behind. He was, he said, lying over the lady in an attempt to shield her, and felt what he described as two blows in the back, like electric shocks.

Opinions seem to be divided as to whether I should send this manuscript to Garth or not. Presuming that I can get it into his hands, which might be difficult, I can see two possible outcomes. Either he is of an open mind in this life, in which case his interest will be piqued and he may be encouraged to meet me, or he will be horrified and I will lose any chance of ever meeting him.

Chapter Nine

I have another interesting account to relate through Madeleine. I find that these recollections that seem to come in the present tense, are more real because of it.

'I know it is another of mother's schemes. It is obvious, as soon as I hear that she has invited my cousins, Dominic and Edward, to stay with us. She is rallying her side of the family to her, in an attempt to try and tear us apart. My cousins are nothing but rude, aggressive bullies and I have never liked them. The last time they came I was only ten years old and they had teased me mercilessly. Even at that innocent age I had struggled to keep my honour when they were near. I had often felt in danger from them.

'My mother never misses any chance to try and destroy what she can never have. Only last night Ryan asked me, his eyes concerned, whether it would be better for me if he left. I was horrified. He told me that she had been saying that she would make both our lives so miserable, that if he truly loved me, he would go for my sake. I responded that he need do only one thing for my sake, and that was to swear he would never leave me. And, perhaps one more thing— He raised his brows questioningly. In answer, I reached out and began to unfasten the buckle of his broad belt. He looked incredulous for a second or two, then he smiled the smile of the wolf. I was indeed growing bold!

'Now, today, Dominic and Edward have arrived, and they are nothing but trouble right from the first moment. Ryan is out working in the fields, so, circumspect, I am keeping to the kitchen, hoping to avoid their menace. But it is not to be. They appear, smiling slyly, in the doorway. They slink into the room like cur dogs, crowding me.

'"Why cousin," Edward begins, "how you have grown. Truly a flower ready to be picked." His insolence is remarkable.

'"Edward - Dominic." I greet them with a curt nod. From the corner of my eye, I can see Nancy bristling like an affronted mother hen. But she must not intervene for the sake of her position.

'"Madeleine," Dominic says, impertinently stroking my cheek with one finger, "our good aunt tells us that you have married below your station. An Irish peasant, is it not?"

'"Ryan is no peasant," I retort. "No more than you or I."

'"But, surely, he is just a boy?" Edward says. "Dominic and I could perhaps give him some advice on matters that only men know of."

'I snort. I cannot help it. The thought of these buffoons instructing Ryan on the manly arts is laughable.

'"Do you laugh at us, Madeleine?" Now Edward's voice has a dangerous tilt.

'"No," I protest, "but now I must leave. I have duties elsewhere." Swiftly, I leave the kitchen, and run upstairs to the safety of my locked bedchamber…

'Now it is noon, and I venture outside to meet Ryan, as is our custom. But as I do so I encounter Dominic. He is standing astride the walkway, effectively barring my way.

'"Please Dominic," I ask, "let me pass. I have to meet my husband."

'"Mmmm," he responds, "I rather like the sound of that. Say 'please Dominic' again. For I could serve you better that a boy from the bogland. A woman like you needs a grown man."

'"Do not be foolish Dominic, you are my cousin," I try.

'"Only by marriage; besides, cousins should show each other affection, do you not agree?" he responds silkily.

'He grows bolder, and lays his hands on my shoulders. I feel only disgust towards him, and I pull away, turning to retrace my steps and find another route. But I see that Edward awaits at the corner. Dominic pulls me back to face him, and putting one hand firmly on my breast, and the other at the back of my neck, he pulls me roughly against him.

'What I have seen, but he has not, is Ryan approaching him quickly from behind. I have never seen Ryan lose his temper so explosively before and it quite frightens me. Almost faster than my eyes can follow, he spins my cousin around, throws him bodily against the wall, pins him there with his fists against Dominic's throat, and draws one hand back to strike him. The primeval rage Ryan is displaying makes me hesitate to touch him, but I grasp his clenched fist and beg him to stop, for I know that this violence is what my mother is hoping for. It is wonderful to me, that at my touch, he is tamed almost instantly. He looks down at me, anger still in his eyes momentarily, then they soften.

'He turns briefly back to Dominic, and says fiercely, "Be sure you never lay hands on her again!" And then, with a contemptuous shove, Ryan pushes him aside, puts his arm around me, and leads me away.

'But Edward has hidden himself from us, and when we reach the corner, both my cousins attack at once. Dominic crashes into Ryan from behind, sending me reeling, and pushing him into Edward, and all three of them end up on the ground. As they scramble to their feet, Edward gets a grip on Ryan from behind, and Dominic takes his opportunity to hit him forcefully in the ribs, causing him to double over, gasping for breath.

'"Come - come!" Dominic leans down and yells in Ryan's face, "Let us see if you have the balls of a man, enough to keep our cousin at home!"

'Ryan explodes once more at this taunt, and he lunges forwards, his head hitting Dominic squarely on the nose, and blood spurts. His weight and momentum drag Edward around too, and he crashes into the wall. This cousin's head is also smeared with blood. It all happens so quickly, that before I know it, Ryan is leading me back inside, leaving my cousins reeling, and cursing him.

'Mother of course blames Ryan, and calls him a bully and a ruffian, but she cannot make him leave. His Irish stubbornness is a match for her cunning…

'As we lay together this night I cannot help but smile. I cannot imagine any other man making me feel this way. Ryan needs no lessons from anyone in the art of pleasuring a woman.'

❧

Meanwhile, back in 1996, life progresses. My young horse is three years old and ready to begin his training under saddle. I am doing all the ground work with him, and then next month he will go to a professional Western yard to be started properly. I am not experienced enough yet to train him in this discipline which is still so new to me.

The time of our holiday in Nashville is also approaching. People who know that I have always been phobic about flying ask me if I am getting really afraid. They really can't believe I am going to cope with the flights. But it won't matter to me how afraid I become, because I'm still going. I know my chances of meeting Garth are very small but I would not forgive myself if I did not take every chance. Therefore being afraid has lost its point so I don't feel afraid.

I read an article about getting over phobias and it tended to advise against what I am planning to do - that is to get on not just one but three planes in one day. They say that flooding a phobia in this way can lead to a nervous breakdown. But I have ultimate faith in two things: first, in that part of me that is Madeleine. She is stronger than me and more adventurous. That part of me will help me to remain calm. The second is my need to get to America. Even if I don't manage to meet Garth, I need to get at least near enough to feel his presence, his reality. This need will give me determination.

❦

There is no date for the following recollection but obviously it was some time after the wedding.

'Another of her pathetic schemes (my mother's) was to force her young maid, who is but twelve years old, to lie naked in our bed. I was expected to find

89

her there and believe that Ryan had betrayed me with her. Sadly for my mother, she had so terrified the poor child by talking of Ryan as if he were some kind of ogre, that when I found her there, she was blubbering with fear and begging me to let her go before he came.'

March 1639

'This evening Ryan and I sit up waiting for the brown mare to foal. The mare is heavy with milk which drips continuously from her. It is a chilly night and outside all is white with frost. Ryan is wearing a rough heavy shirt. It reaches to his mid-thigh. This is covered by a woollen cloak. He has brown breeches and brown boots. I am wearing a grey work dress and black boots. My hair is bound up in a white cap, but as usual after a few minutes with Ryan, my hair is loose - he so prefers it this way.

'We lay, comfortably propped in the deep straw, both wrapped in Ryan's cloak. We are just outside the mare's stall in the barn. I am at Ryan's left side and he has his left arm around me. His right arm is across me and he holds my right hand in his. I lean against his chest, feeling so safe here. I can feel the texture of his shirt against my cheek, and I can hear his strong and regular heartbeat and feel the heat of his skin. The air smells sweet and warm in the barn. I can hear the mare breathing deeply in the stall. Ryan has witnessed this event many times before in Ireland, but not I. It is one of the things denied to a lady, and yet one more reason, no doubt, for disapproval. After a while, lulled by the warmth of Ryan's arms, and the rhythm of his heart, I fall asleep.

'Later, I am not sure how much later, he awakens me by gently stroking my cheek. He puts a finger to my lips to warn me to remain silent so as not to startle the mare. She is lying down now, breathing heavily and groaning softly. Ryan points out to me the small bulge under the mare's tail. He whispers to me that it is the foal's front feet. As the mare strains rhythmically, so the foal's legs are pushed outwards in time with her. Soon I can see a tiny muzzle peeping from between the legs.

'Suddenly, the mare lurches to her feet, and the violent movement causes the foal to be propelled from her body, until the weight of it drops it clear of her, onto the straw. The mare immediately turns to the foal, making deep whickering noises. I find my eyes filling up with tears as the miracle takes place. Ryan gets up and quietly enters the stall, speaking gently to her. He clears the birth membrane from the foal's muzzle, so that it may breathe easily, and then he returns to my side. The mare begins to lick her colt. The miracle continues, as the colt, like a drunken sop, tries to stand on its spindly legs. Eventually he gains his feet and, still staggering, manages to find his mother's milk, beginning to suck greedily.

'Ryan says we may leave now, if we wish, and return to our warm bed, but we stay until morning. I will never forget this night, lying safe and warm within the shelter of his arms as we burrow cosily together in the straw, listening to the contented sounds of this tiny new life and his joyful mother. Sometimes I sleep for a while, then half awaken briefly to savour this precious time before drifting back to sleep in utter contentment. I know we were born to be together. No-one will ever part us, this I swear. Should they try, then I shall wither and die, like a tree severed from its roots…

'The next day there is snow. It covers the ground more deeply than I have ever seen before. We are both feeling the exhilaration of witnessing the new life so that we play in the snow like excited children. We begin throwing balls of snow at each other. My skill is superior to Ryan's. His throws have much more force behind them but mine more often find their target, so soon Ryan is covered in snow. In mock fury he runs at me and tumbles me into a snow bank. Then he pushes handfuls of the icy snow down the neck of my gown. I squeal and struggle but he is stronger and pins me there mercilessly. Eventually, when he feels I have paid enough, he pulls me to my feet, and putting me across his shoulder, he carries me, still squealing, into the kitchen.

'Nancy stares at us aghast. Then as Ryan puts me down, she begins to fuss over us, pulling us both over to the fire. She brings to us hot spiced wine, and soon we are warm, our faces glowing in the firelight. I can feel my cheeks burning as the sensation returns to them. Ryan's face is ruddy with the light from the flames, and the heat from the snow, and his eyes at this moment are so alive, so blue - his dark hair accentuating them - that they take on the colour of a peacock's breast.' [Madeleine actually called the bird a peafowl, but I changed the word to give you a better idea of the colour she referred to.]

Chapter Ten

Back in the present time, I have found two new song co-writers, and things are looking very promising. Also, I have become the booking agent for a Country Music band called 'Stealer' who have recorded one of my songs. This is keeping me fairly busy and we are having a lot of good nights out with them.

Tony has offered to take me to Hambledon, to look at church records, houses, and even cemeteries. It must be very odd indeed if you ever find yourself standing at your own grave. One of the problems we have is that my subconscious is unable to dredge up Madeleine's maiden name. That makes things much more difficult. I am wondering whether the fact that I have been shown the portraits means that this is the direction I should be looking in for proof of this story. So I have placed an advertisement in a magazine that specialises in tracing ancestors. I have asked for any historical facts relating to Madeleine or Ryan, or, best of all, a portrait of either of them. I know it's a long shot, but how wonderful it would be if I could find something.

How do you get close to someone like Garth? It seems to me that it is impossible unless you either live in Nashville (who knows - one day!) and meet quite by accident or it comes about through his choice. For him to choose, first he must know I exist. I have discovered that a letter is out of the question. No mail is accepted at his home; it is all redirected to his management offices where once again it hits a wall of blanket responses. Out of interest, a very good friend of mine, Hannah Valise, who is a journalist and has met Garth on about ten occasions - I know; sickening, isn't it! - has told me that I wouldn't need to ask for a hug. She says that Garth is a compulsive hugger.

The only remaining possibilities I can see at the moment are through a chance meeting or at a concert. Garth does make himself very accessible to people who happen to be in the right place at the right time, but pinning him down is notoriously difficult. I feel that is because he is naturally unpredictable - he loves to surprise people. Always supposing we could get to a concert, he does often meet some fans afterwards. Whether you have to be chosen in some way or whether it's just whoever waits the longest, I don't know. Obviously if that were the case, I'd wait as long as necessary. Have you ever thought about how frustrating it must be to have someone that you love desperately so out of your reach; to have no control or influence over their fate; to have no knowledge, from one minute to the next, of their personal well-being or safety? And to live in the constant fear of an impersonal item on the news informing you someday of their fate? It's horrible.

I think I have finally discovered the truth about where Ryan died. It had crossed my mind, rather horribly, to wonder what happened to his body after he died. I try not to dwell on it as I find it very upsetting. But I decided to dowse over a map for an answer as to where he fell. I think they made shore at Sunderland. There were probably meant to meet the army at Newcastle; then, while making their way back to the ship, (as I have said before) I believe they were killed near Lumley Castle. I made a rough drawing of this castle. One day perhaps I will go there but there is no way I am spiritually strong enough yet. If I have managed to see Garth at a later date then I may be able to cope with it OK. Ryan and Madeleine loved each other so much; I think anyone reading this tale will be aware of that by now. I still grieve for their loss. As Madeleine, I never got the chance to grieve for Ryan properly. It has been suggested to me that I light two candles for them and have a small personal ceremony in order to say goodbye to them both. I will find that very emotional. It may well be over three hundred years in the past, but my memories are new, so to me it is like yesterday. Even the thought of this farewell brings tears to my eyes.

I also feel guilty that, as Madeleine, I hadn't done something to avoid this tragedy. I had had plenty of opportunity to see the danger coming. I really thought at the time that we would be able to act quickly enough to avoid disaster. But, as we all learn at some point, it only takes a minute to ruin it all. A lapse of attention while driving or crossing the road is all it takes to change everything for us. Life is precarious. It's bad enough when you only have yourself to worry about, but, as soon as you love someone else, be it mate or child, you have more in your life; you have so much more to lose too. As Madeleine, I learned that, for all my hopes and good intentions, within mere seconds others had intervened, and both our lives were destroyed almost before we could register what was going on. Suddenly Ryan was gone, and she was helpless. There was nothing she could do then; it was too late. I try to tell myself that she was only seventeen, where could they have gone? If she had left her father's house she would have immediately lost all claim to his support. They would have had nowhere to live. But I wish that, as Madeleine, I had at least tried. Anything at all would have been better than what happened.

This is what happened immediately after Madeleine was released from her prison room after two days and nights of captivity - a time during which she truly thought she would go out of her mind with anguish. I think there was a point when she would have even welcomed insanity as a way of escaping her torment.

Late May 1640 (Ryan was taken on twentieth May 1640)

'I spent many days down at the docks having begged rides in passing carriages. All I knew was that Ryan had been taken to a ship. When it rained I spent some time huddled miserably under a hand cart with a street waif for company. It was warm or I would surely have died from exposure and lack of nourishment. I was very fortunate not to be attacked by some drunken varlet, although in truth, I was long past caring about what happened to me. All the daytime I roamed from ship to ship, taunted by crude remarks from the seamen while I searched for a trace of Ryan. But I think I knew it was useless right from the start. Eventually Father sent some men to fetch me back. At the house I sent out despatches to everyone I could think of who might take pity on me, but the world was sealed against me.'

Chapter Eleven

Today (1996), quite by chance, I caught part of a TV programme where someone was doing almost the same thing my friend had suggested I do for Ryan and Madeleine; that was to hold a short ceremony to say goodbye. The girl in the programme was saying goodbye to a child she had lost in a miscarriage. She was feeling guilty about the baby not having the life she had been promised, and she was saying sorry to her. Suddenly I found tears welling in my own eyes, and myself saying, 'I'm so sorry Ryan,' over and over again.

Obviously it is not just the grief I have to deal with here. Now that Madeleine has completely returned to me I have revealed all the suppressed guilt she suffered - that I have suffered. Maybe this guilt is the reason I have never felt deserving of all my blessings. I was thinking of how Ryan died and feeling very sorry for the pain he had to endure, all because of me. I played no direct part in hurting him, but if he hadn't loved me he would have moved on, and his death would never have happened that way. Maybe this is why I have always found it hard to accept that Tony loves me now. Perhaps I think loving me will cause something bad to happen to him too.

Poor Ryan was also well aware of the sort of thing that might happen to him if he stayed where he was hated so much. As Madeleine, I totally underestimated how evil Margaret was, and I thought, naïvely, that we could control the situation. Ryan did not. He did try to persuade me to leave sometimes. I must have been really stupid.

On that fateful day when Ryan was taken from me, that last look that we exchanged, almost spoke, for his part, of accepting what he had always known was inevitable. After that long gaze of desperation, he turned his head away sadly, in a gesture of nigh on resignation. That is not to say he wasn't willing to fight for us. The dreadful sounds that came from the hall showed that he was attempting to fight the three men it took to drag him out. And when I saw him from the upstairs window he had been knocked senseless so they had obviously had a job to subdue him. I know that he would have taken the smallest chance to escape if any had arisen. It was just as if his worst fears had come true as he had always known they would. This forms a major part of the reason I need to talk to him one day about this. I really need to know just what he was thinking.

But I have been distracted. What I must make Madeleine's spirit understand is that the blame lies squarely on her parents - on her stepmother for her evil vindictive nature, and on her father for being too weak to stop what he knew was wrong. All I ever did as Madeleine was to love Ryan with all my heart and soul, and perhaps be a little naïve - there can't be any sin involved there.

If I decide to go ahead with the ceremony I will have to be alone, both to complete it and to recover from it afterwards. What I do feel compelled to do, every day, is to listen to some of Garth's music or watch him for a while on one of the few pieces of video film of him that I have managed to collect. Unfortunately there is only one video of him for sale in this country. The others I have are short clips I have taped from TV appearances, award ceremonies, etc., plus, of course, the tape of the original concert that started it all. It is very nice and very necessary to see these but sometimes it makes my heart ache with the need to see him for real. Discovering all this latent guilt makes me wonder if part of this enormous need comes from my desire to be forgiven by him for letting him down in that past life.

I have one clip of him singing without his cowboy gear. It makes no difference to me. Once he starts singing he just draws me into the emotions of the song. It was very interesting though that he chose to appear this way in a rare British TV appearance. Quite a few of my friends saw him for the first time that day, and they were expecting some loud cowboy. He is renowned for liking to surprise people, and so he didn't give them what they were expecting. He was dressed in normal casual gear, no hat of course, and he sang a very gentle ballad (which I am sure was inspired by his wife - it sounds just like her). It was also obvious to those of us that are familiar with him that he was not, contrary to appearances, singing in front of a live audience. An audience changes him - and this time it didn't happen. A friend of mine made me smile. When I asked her if she thought he was quiet on the show she said, 'Well, he's not an extrovert is he?' I didn't correct her, but, boy, is she in for a shock one of these days!

Chapter Twelve

We had planned to take very few clothes with us to Nashville, but an empty suitcase for new gear. Clothes are always a problem for me. I never feel that I look good in anything. I had to remind myself that Garth was no longer Ryan, and so even if we met it wouldn't matter how I looked to him. It was the person inside that mattered.

The months turned into weeks, the weeks into days.

The advert I had placed began to bear fruit. A man phoned to say that he had a portrait which could possibly be of Ryan. Although the portrait was not named, and was by a minor artist, the age of the subject, his hair and clothes, seemed to be right. I had taken steps to avoid trickery by not mentioning them in the advert. Obviously I would recognise him if I saw the painting, so I asked the man to send me a photo of it.

The photo came - it was not Ryan. This was a huge disappointment.

I had another call, this time from an art dealer. This time I was very cautious, thinking that he might be looking for an easy sale. But he told me that he had a portrait of Ryan Fitzgerald. The hook that I swallowed was that it was a pastel and not the usual oil painting. Surely, this time I was going to be lucky. But the man was suspiciously unhelpful. He was not willing to take a photo of the portrait and send it to me. He said that it was for sale, right now, and if I wanted it I would have to pay the full asking price of £2000. I asked him many questions concerning the year, the age of the subject, the clothes, the colour of hair and eyes. And they all seemed to match what Madeleine had shown me. But £2000 was a lot to gamble. I knew Tony wouldn't approve, quite sensibly, and a trip to Hampshire, where it was, was out of the question at that moment. I really couldn't expect my whole family to make sacrifices, and rearrange their priorities on the basis of such a risk. I felt Madeleine encouraging me. Supposing it was sold to someone else while I still dithered?

In the end, I decided on a compromise, something I could live with. I decided to send £50 as a non-returnable deposit. That way if it was a confidence trick, and anyone would think that it was, I would only lose £50 and not £2000. I knew I was being foolish - why wouldn't he send me the photo? (In hindsight I can see that he wouldn't have understood how I would recognise this person from 1639.) Anyway suppose it was genuine? I had to do something.

But, as I had feared might happen, I got another call from the dealer, Mr Maycock, to say that the picture had been sold before my cheque arrived. I expected him to go on to say he would let me have it if I paid more than the purchaser, but it seemed I had misjudged him. As far as he was concerned it was sold - end of story. I was devastated. I still didn't know, of course, if it was Ryan for sure - but now that I couldn't have it - I was convinced that it was him. Then Mr Maycock gave me a ray of hope. Although he wasn't prepared to reconsider the sale he told me that the picture would remain in his storeroom for a couple of days while the new owners moved house. In that time he was prepared to have a copy done by a local artist for the £50 I had already sent plus another £50. Again it was a risk. I had to accept that it very likely wasn't Ryan anyway. But what could I do? What would you have done? So I agreed.

When the portrait came, I could hardly dare open it. But it was Ryan…I couldn't believe it. Tears, of joy this time, streamed down my face accompanied by a big smile. I felt as if I had achieved something truly wonderful. Madeleine was overjoyed. If I had given in to her I would have sat staring at this face from the past all day long. At some point I will have to confess to Tony what I have done - I can never keep a secret from him for long.

I can't explain how wonderful it is to have this portrait. It makes everything so much more vivid in my memory. Though of course some bad memories are made worse by it. It is worth it, though, to have this image of Ryan in front of my eyes, instead of only inside my head. He is exactly as I pictured him. As for other people the resemblance to Garth, as he is today, sends shivers down their spines. I wish I could show it to him.

Of course, once again with hindsight, I would have paid anything for the original had I known it was really Ryan. But that's easy to say now that I know it is. Mr Maycock would not give me the new owner's names - I think he began to find me a little strange. When a little time has passed, I may try again.

103

We went to Hambledon a few weeks later and we found such a lot of proof. We started with our search for ***** House. Oddly, no-one in the village shop could tell us where it was, and we began to get desperate. Then I realised that I didn't need any help. I remembered clearly that it lay on a route north-east out of the village so we used the car compass to find a road that led north-east, and followed it. After about a mile we drove around a bend and there it was. I have to say that I wasn't one hundred per cent sure for a moment or two. First, there was no name plate, and second, although the tower end that I had described to Tony was there, the house looked slightly wrong. Then I realised why. The black diamond-paned leaded windows had been replaced with white windows that looked to be more likely Georgian to me. Likewise the heavy oak studded door had been replaced. The grounds had also changed. The driveway used to be longer and the garden denser. I told Tony that I was now sure it was the right house. There was no option but to knock and ask if I was right. I had been afraid that my emotions would take me over to the point where the owners would think I was deranged and not let us anywhere near. But something or someone had kindly 'switched me off' and I felt calm and numb.

It was, said the lady owner, ***** House. She was very kind and allowed us to walk around outside and take some photos. We told her our ancestors had lived there - just a tiny white lie to avoid any embarrassment to her or us. The first thing that I noticed was the unusual feature of the narrow slitted window of the room where Madeleine was held prisoner while they took Ryan away. Then I remembered, looking up, that Nancy had slept in the highest storey of the tower and that Ryan and Madeleine's bedchamber was one floor below. I was careful not to peer into any of the windows, partly out of respect for the owners' privacy and partly because I didn't want to trigger my emotions.

At the rear of the property the old windows remained and it all looked much more familiar, although the back gardens are tiny compared with the old ones. I was able to point out to Tony the attic window that Madeleine climbed out from before she jumped from the roof. Most sweet to me is that the barn where Ryan slept before our marriage is still there, right across from the kitchen door, just as I had described. The courtyard in between, though, has either been removed or covered with a lawn. I just had to peer inside the barn. Oh, the pictures that flashed through my mind! Sadly at that point we were interrupted by the lady owner. I think she had begun to worry that maybe we were burglars casing the joint! So we left. But not before we found out that the attic has a reputation for being haunted. Well it did - but I'd be willing to bet that the ghost has mysteriously disappeared since our visit!

There were only remnants of the woodland that had been behind the house but the meadow below is still there, and so is the footpath that leads to the old green lane. I did not want to go down to the lane, lest I re-experience the scene of the beating that nearly killed Ryan (more later). So with a last look over my shoulder, as the house dwindled into the distance, we left ***** House and drove back into

Hambledon to look in the cemeteries. We could find no trace of Madeleine being buried in the local graveyard, and the church records were not available, but we did find a rather sad, unmarked grave just outside the main confines of the churchyard. I was a little scared as I stood over the mound, but I felt no goosebumps, just a warm glow. This surprised me but I was sure this was where Madeleine lay. As a suicide from a Catholic family she may not have been allowed to lie in consecrated ground. Anyway, we bought a large bunch of red roses and placed them there. The card read, 'Torn apart but together for all time. Ryan'.

The time of our trip draws closer. I had written a set of lyrics that I desperately wanted to get to Garth. The song was called *The Scent of a Rose*, and I felt he would really relate to the words. No-one in the industry would believe me I'm sure but it really wasn't about money or kudos. I just wanted some of my words to reach him. No-one would sing these words like he could, and I wouldn't care if I never got a penny.

I was also continuing to train my young horse in a method called PNH - Parelli Natural Horsemanship. Pat Parelli, was the inventor of the system and I considered him to be a genius.

The Scent of a Rose

Sometimes I can almost forget her face
And the way her eyes and mine embraced
Then that special scent fills the evening breeze
And once more I find myself down on my knees

Chorus

The scent of roses fills the air at night
That's when I always lose the fight
I try to be strong but when darkness grows
I'm helpless against the scent of a rose

I can forget the sound her laughter made
The touch of her hand begins to fade
Then I catch the scent of a rose in bloom
And once again she's there in the room

It's hard to believe that something so sweet
Has the power to knock me off my feet

The way she moved sometimes slips from my mind
And the summer sun sometimes makes me blind
But my eyes can see and I have to cry
When the scent of a rose fills the night sky

The portrait triggered a new memory. This event did not have any direct bearing on Madeleine and Ryan's fate, but it is important to me. It helped to show me that life, anyone's life, is precarious to say the least, and that we are always living on a knife edge. That is why I think that it seems as if their lives were very intense - they really 'lived for the moment'. Today we tend to feel safer; we think we have plenty of time - time to say what we really mean to loved ones, time to heal a rift. But we don't. Today on a news programme there was an item about a light aircraft falling on a woman as she walked her dog on a beach. How do you prepare for something like that? Unexpected tragedy waits around every corner. Do it today, you don't know how many tomorrows you might have.

This event took place in the high summer of either 1638, or 1639. Perhaps a history book could tell me which.

'The horses picked their way through the powdery remains of burnt branches littering the track. Grey puffs of ash plumed from every hoof as it hit the ground. It would have been impossible to travel at anything faster than a walking pace without becoming enveloped in a choking cloud. Looking around at the destruction I was amazed to think that I had survived the inferno. I reached across to touch Ryan's hand as he rode beside me in unspoken thanks that we were both alive. He too looked stunned at the extent of the damage done to the forest. Pitiful bundles of charred bones and fur marked the tragic passing of the dozens of creatures which had lived in the undergrowth. They had been mercilessly incinerated as the fire swept along the forest floor.

'The events had happened two days since and had begun at first light when I had awoken to find Ryan missing from my side. It was not unusual for him to rise early for work but normally he would not have left without saying goodbye. I dressed and hurried downstairs but the house appeared empty, there being no noise from any quarter. Nancy was not in the kitchen and the first person I came across was my father, who was pacing anxiously in the gardens. I asked him if he knew where Ryan had gone and he told me that all the men and household servants had been roused in the night to go and help fight a terrible fire that had broken out in a neighbour's house. They had been gone since four o' clock in the morning when it had been pitch dark. He pointed to the south and, indeed, I could see a black pall of smoke hanging over the treetops. Father said that the men were required at home now for the cows were lowing pathetically, needing to be relieved of their milk. But Father feared that the fire had by then raged out of control and eaten into the tinder dry forest, for there had been no real rainfall for months. And if it had then that would be a real disaster.

'As he spoke, the first weary returning band appeared out of the woods. Their faces and clothes were blackened with soot and dust but I could still see that Ryan was not among them. I hurried toward them to enquire as to his whereabouts. They told us that the fire had indeed spread into the forest and was now out of control. But what of Ryan? I asked them again. It transpired that the band had split up and that Ryan was with those who had elected to stay on whilst this group had returned for milking. Next, Nancy and the other servants came back, also dirty and exhausted. They told us that, sadly, they had been unable to save anyone at the house, and that it had burned to the ground. I asked Nancy if she had seen anything of Ryan but she had not. She told me that chaos reigned at the scene of the fire, with no real organisation in evidence.

'Two more hours passed and still there was no sign of the rest of our men. The black cloud hovered more thickly over the green of the woodland, like some giant evil bird of prey. There was at least no danger to our estate for the wind was blowing the fire away from us.

Finally I could wait no longer. I have always been an impulsive person, and waiting, to me, was the worst torture. Secretly, for I knew they would try to stop me had they known, I saddled a horse and set off to find Ryan. Had I but curbed my impetuous spirit for one more hour I would have had Ryan come home safe to me.

'I was still some way from the heart of the conflagration when my horse became nervous, prancing and snorting in fear. At that point I met the rest of Father's men making their weary way home. Ryan was not with them and now my heart began to shiver. The men were in a poor condition, coughing and staggering from the effects of the smoke, tendrils of which were creeping through the trees, even at this distance from the blaze. I was dismayed to learn that Ryan had been sent with the other most able men to open a firebreak ahead of the flames, further south. It had been decided that the fire could not be quenched, and so a firebreak was the only way to save further acreage from destruction. This involved cutting a swathe through the trees, leaving the fire nothing to feed on when it reached this gap. The firebreak was being created some distance to the south, and to get there I would have to ride around the extremes of the fire. I could not return home without seeing Ryan. Seeing him was the only way I could soothe my fearful heart.

'I came soon upon the burnt remains of our neighbours' house. It was hard to imagine that a house full of people had ever stood in that ghastly place. Only a handful of people were about, sifting through the still-smouldering embers. I told them that I was heading for the firebreak, and they thought I would be safe enough if I passed to the west of the fire, so I set off in confident spirits. But I can only imagine that the wind must have changed its direction suddenly, for after a while there came a great roaring sound, drawing ever closer. It sounded like a speeding wind or hail on a roof. I realised that it was not wind or hail that I could hear, only the crackling sound of flames. It was terrifying. The air around me seemed to become rare, and it stung my

110

throat. I could not seem to draw in enough breath to satisfy my lungs. Then my horse became difficult to control, her heart beating as frantically as mine. She began to whinny anxiously and plunged, trying to flee. Eventually I could control her no longer and I dismounted, for I was afraid that in her fear and confusion she would carry me back towards the fire. I had heard of horses which returned to their burning stables, after they had been rescued from them.

'My eyes began to water profusely and, although I turned away from the direction of the noise and where the air quivered with heat haze, the fire seemed to be travelling much faster than I had thought possible. I began to cough and this weakened my grip so that, when the horse leapt and snatched at the reins, I was unable to hold on and she broke away. I wished then I had stayed on her back for she galloped away at great speed and went, after all, in the direction of safety. I was really terrified now. I was in a part of the forest that I did not know well and I had no idea in which direction to go. The noise of the fire was horrifying and the heat seemed to be all around me now. I struggled onwards, feeling tiny and slow in a forest grown huge. I felt as if I were wading through knee-high mud whilst death stalked me on giant fiery legs, devouring the earth behind me with its huge strides. I dared not turn to see how close it was, for I could feel its hot fingers on the back of my head.

'I do not know how long I staggered onwards through the ever-thickening smoke. I became weak and dizzy, my breathing laboured. I remember that, at one point, a deer ran past me on wings of fear, not even glancing at me, her former predator, for I was now more helpless than her against nature's most powerful weapon. I could hardly breathe at

111

all now and the air rasped in my throat. I began to despair. I tripped and fell, and was truly tempted just to lie there and let fate overtake me, for even the as yet unburnt trees ahead of me had red blooms sparking high in their branches. Thoughts of Ryan brought me to my feet. I could not leave him. On I went once more, almost blind, just moving away from the heat at my back. Smoke swirled around me and my eyes were running with tears.

After a few more long minutes I was so hot that I feared my hair or clothes would soon ignite and I began to scream out. This was what saved me. Unbeknownst to me Ryan was close by. He had finally returned to the house when the wind had changed and it was obvious that their efforts at creating a firebreak were worthless. He had skirted the eastern side of the fire with the other men. The wind was driving the fire west, and it was the turn of the men from the villages in that direction to build their own firebreak. Of course, when he reached home our roles were reversed for I was the missing one. Ryan set off to find me immediately, taking Father's best horse, his actions for once finding no objections with my parents. He rode to the burnt-out house and fortunately was told where I had gone. It was as well that he was a much stronger rider than I and therefore more able to control his mount when it became afraid.

'He was becoming extremely desperate, he told me later, but unable to accept the possibility that the fire had overtaken me. His imagination constantly created phantoms in the swirling smoke which he convinced himself were me, only to see them drift apart as he came nearer. Then he heard me crying out. When he appeared, clad in a grey veil of smoke, from between the trees, I thought for a moment that

112

he was a vision brought on by wishful thinking and the poisonous fumes. But he rode his horse up close, then reached down with arms of flesh and blood to lift me onto the horse in front of him. He did not speak for there was no air to spare. There followed a breakneck dash which I have no desire ever to repeat. I was perched sideways on the horse; there was no side-saddle to hold me in place while I was crouched low over its sweating neck, flecks of foam from its mouth flying in my face. I would have tumbled off if it had not been for Ryan's arms preventing me as they reached around me to grasp the reins. I could feel his legs driving the horse forcefully on, his hands guiding firmly, making sure the panicked animal stayed on its course to safety. In truth it needed little urging to run - for fear was its master. Branches flashed by, frighteningly close to our heads; only Ryan's steady hands on the reins saving us from collision.

'Eventually we found ourselves in clean, sweet air. It was so wonderful to breathe easily again, to breathe in cool air that did not sear the lungs. And now I could also see again. It seemed almost miraculous to see whole green trees instead of blackened burnt stumps of charcoal. Gradually Ryan slowed the horse to a trot, then a walk. We had outflanked the fire. The poor horse was very tired. Its coat slowly dried, leaving streaks of white salt from the sweat amongst the black sooty smears. Ryan brought it to a halt and slid off. He stared up at me speechlessly for a moment as if he did not quite believe his eyes. Then he held up his arms and lifted me down from the panting horse. It was then that I realised the full extent of Ryan's exhaustion, for he sank suddenly and helplessly to the ground, so that I ended up in his lap. He stayed there, rocking me in his arms, soothing both our frantic hearts. We still did not speak - there seemed no adequate words - but after a while I began to cough and shiver, and Ryan took off his smudged and dirty shirt to put about me. Then our blessed mount carried me home with Ryan walking at its head.'

1996

The most important thing on my mind was getting to Nashville, and hopefully, getting near to Garth. Getting to Nashville alone seemed like a miracle to me, as I had never experienced the speed of air travel before.

While the countdown seemed to take forever, when the day came to leave it seemed to arrive in a rush. Before I knew it we were packed, in the car and on our way to the airport. It was only five a.m. but, believe me, I was well awake! Passing through airport security was interesting, speaking as one who has never been admitted through those mysterious portals before. Before I knew it we were at the bottom of the steps. (Just to add difficulty to my nervous condition we were travelling to a major airport, Amsterdam, from our local one at Norwich. This meant no concealing tunnels and no pretending it was a bus! No; we had actually to walk out across the tarmac and up steps into the plane.) The plane looked too big ever to get off the ground and yet too small to be safe. It was also a propeller plane, not a jet. I went up the steps ahead of Tony, and a part of me (I expect you know which part) made me turn round to him and smile broadly into his anxious face.

I know that up to then Tony had still had his doubts as to whether or not I would be able to do it at all - therefore his expression when I smiled at him was hilarious. I was scared. But I took a deep breath, remembering what Ryan and Madeleine had gone through to be together, and in I went. As I sat down I felt that terrified part of me receding into some small safe place in the centre of my being. Madeleine was taking over as I knew she would. It was surprisingly small inside the plane but more comfortable than I had imagined. When it took off I actually enjoyed it. I have never been one for fairground rides but I enjoyed the power of the aircraft. The only moment that took my breath away was when we reached our correct altitude. At that point some power comes off, the aircraft seems to slow down and you wonder if its going to stay up there!

It was rather worrying to have to land and take off again, not only in Amsterdam, but again in Detroit, but we made it. On the flight between Amsterdam and Detroit we did experience some turbulence. At this time I retreated into the past and believed myself to be travelling along a road in a bumpy horse and cart - a useful device if you ever find yourself in that position. Between the meals and drinks I had plenty of time to meditate. I had some of my clearest images there. Let me explain that the clearer the airwaves are around you, the clearer the signal is. This is why important messages seem to come at night when the people around you are asleep. Otherwise you can get annoying interference, just like on a TV or radio. And this means there are sometimes irritating gaps which you have to try and fill in.

Chapter Thirteen

As you can probably imagine then, flying through clear air, at however many thousands of feet we were, with only the odd satellite signal and air traffic control to worry about, any meditations are very clear. So, for the first time, and I had been trying all along, I finally saw Ryan and Madeleine's wedding day. The first thing I saw was a very sharp picture of them walking hand in hand along a grassy lane; then an image of them, looking very small, inside a rather grand looking church. The church had stone vaulted ceilings and an ornately carved stone altar. This surprised me as I had thought that they must have been married in some tiny back street place.

However the unexpected setting was explained when I discovered the name of the church. It was Milton Abbey church which, of course, by that year (1638) was disused, the abbeys all having been closed by Henry VIII. I will let Madeleine tell the story.

April 1638

'We rode all day to reach our destination. Ryan was taking me to Milton Abbey, and we intended to make use of the disused church there. Ryan knew of it for he had had employment and had lived on a farm in the village of Charlton Marshall, not far away. It was to this farm that he first took me. We were greeted warmly by the farmer's family, but I was immediately a little jealous of the daughter, Marian. She greeted Ryan a little too familiarly for my liking, throwing her arms around him and kissing him soundly. She was very comely, plump, with dark, curly hair, brown eyes and a very red mouth. Ryan was however, quick to pay heed to my discomfiture and stepped away from her. Putting his arm around me instead, he drew me forward to meet her. She looked me over a little disdainfully but I paid her no more heed. If she coveted Ryan I could not blame her.

'Ryan left me at the farm, and disappeared in the direction of the Abbey. He was gone all evening, and half the night. The farmer had kindly allowed us the use of his hay barn for the night and I was already asleep when Ryan returned. I awoke briefly in my makeshift bed of hay to feel him flop down beside me in exhaustion. Within seconds we were both fast asleep.

'We were woken early in the morning by the farmer coming to feed his stock. Ryan was buoyed up with excitement. I had feared that he might have involved Nancy in some way, and might be risking her position. But he had not been so foolish. He showed me now that he only had Nancy's own wedding band which she had given to him for me to use. Her own husband was long since dead. It warmed my heart to think of her sacrifice. Ryan had, since I had known him, worn a gold ring on a cord around his neck. I had been amazed that through all his trials and tribulations, he had never let anyone steal it, or been tempted to sell it to help himself. It had been his father's, and now he intended to use it for his own. Neither of us had any ceremonial clothes to wear. We were both dressed in our normal attire, and Ryan was a little dusty from his mysterious secret labours. However I had woven a crown for my hair out of spring flowers wrapped around a circlet made from a hazel wand.

'We rode to the Abbey church, and arrived there at eight o' clock. When we entered the church I could not believe the beautiful sight Ryan had created for me. Somehow - I do not know how - he had filled the area around the altar with wild flowers, bunches and bunches of them, and there must have been fifty candles, in stone sconces, burning in a half circle around the altar itself. I turned to him, my eyes pricking with tears; I truly loved him so much that it almost hurt. His eyes too smouldered with a love not to be denied. We made our way under the vaulted ceiling, to the altar. There stood a rather anxious looking man of the clergy, the farmer and his family. The ceremony was short, of necessity, but perfect even so. The church looked like a magic cave, with the flickering pools created by the candles and the blue and yellow of all the flowers. I needed no more proof of his love, or he mine, but we made our own vows.

Madeleine's vow:-

'There is no one who owns me, and therefore no-one who can give me. Therefore I give myself to you, with no part held back. You will know every part of me, even to my soul. I will never deceive you, and I will never have a secret from you. I will love you forever, for I cannot help myself.

Ryan's vow:-

'I will defend you with my body, and I will love you with my soul. I will never deceive you, and I will never leave you while I still breathe. I will protect you from all others, even unto laying down my life at your feet. My life is yours for the taking.

'Such was my happiness that I did not flinch when Marian took her opportunity to kiss Ryan once more. We set off immediately to face the trouble we knew would inevitably be waiting for us at home. I had harboured hopes that Mother and Father might accept the deed once it was done. But my prayers were in vain. We knew that they would have been concerned when we did not return home on the yester evening, and thought they might have guessed what we were about. We were right; they had guessed but their reactions were worse than I ever imagined.

❦

[I interrupt here, to tell you that when we returned to England, after our holiday, we paid another flying visit to Hampshire, to take our son's belongings back to his digs at university. While we were there we detoured into Dorset to pay a visit to Milton Abbey and to see where Ryan and Madeleine were married. It was a long detour but I kept remembering the way that Ryan had persuaded her that it was worth the trouble because the church was so beautiful, that he had decided as soon as he saw it that, should he ever wed, then he wanted it to be there. He was right; the very sight of this wonderful church brought tears to my eyes. But before we saw the church, I should point out that when we drove through the village of Milton Abbas, I told Tony that the village was wrong. Today the village runs along both sides of one main street and there is little else but back in 1638 it was a complex cluster of dwellings, all mixed together in a jumble. Some houses, well hovels really, were back to back, with a tangle of paths and animal pens in between. One of the things we saw inside the church was a painting of how the village used to be before a fire destroyed it, and before it was rebuilt in its current form. The original village was just as I had described. The church lies in a bowl, surrounded by wooded slopes. It is ornately shaped but looks to have grown there almost naturally rather than to have been built by the hands of man.

Turning the old latch, and opening the heavy wooden door, was very strange. When I walked inside it was like stepping into another world. The stone vaulted ceiling is just as I described, and I walked up the aisle and stood where I had as Madeleine all those years ago. The altar area, as I had remembered, is highly carved from floor to ceiling. The most amazing thing of all concerns my memory of the semi-circle of candles around the altar. For in the carved stone wall, at intervals of about a foot, there are sconces. And on the day that we were at the church there were actually candles in the sconces, just as there had been on Ryan and Madeleine's wedding day. I have never seen this feature in any other church. My emotions in this place were unchecked, in contrast to the visit to ***** House, and I could not help tears pouring down my cheeks as I stood there. On one level, I could feel Ryan's presence next to me, shoulder to shoulder with me, but on another level, I felt so alone because he wasn't really there. Tony, in complete and amazing understanding, had stayed at the back of the church, leaving me alone with my thoughts. Now he joined me and I clung to him gratefully. It was a wonderful place and I will never forget it - or Ryan.]

'We were summoned to the drawing room. Father stood at the mantle leaning on his stick, looking sick and weary. He said not one word. Mother was scarlet with pent-up rage. She marched over to us and pushed with both hands against Ryan's chest in fury, trying to make him move from my side where he stood. Then she turned her back on him, and addressed me.

'"Madeleine! What have you done?" she demanded.

'I held out my left hand to show her my ring. "Ryan and I are wed," I answered.

'"No!" she screamed. She clutched at my outstretched hand and tried to pull the ring off. I snatched my hand back in a fist. No-one would ever remove this symbol of our joining unless they first severed my hand.

'"You idiot child!" she hissed. "You have been promised to Joseph Pennington, that good man of London, for years. Do you understand what you have given up—" she pointed at Ryan "—for this!"

'"I have given up nothing," I retorted, taking hold of Ryan's hand. "You, maybe, have lost the prestige you desire above all else, of having the Pennington name associated with your family. And you will miss your daughter becoming the heir to a fortune. I have escaped being tied to an old man for whom I have

121

no use! And I am wed to the only man I will ever love! You will never know such love!"

'She was so enraged by this truth, that she drew back her hand to slap me.

'Ryan stepped forward and grasped her wrist, "No," he said, pushing her arm down with quiet force. She snatched her hand away, turning to face him with undisguised disgust in her face.

'"You dare to lay hands on me!" she screamed at him. "You insolent scoundrel! Know this! You will never be a son to me!"

'"Nor Madam," he responded, "would I ever wish to be."

'At this insult she brought her arm swinging round and slapped Ryan on the face with all the force she could muster. This time he made no attempt to stop her but stood unmoving as the shape of her splayed fingers flamed red on his cheek. His eyes met hers steadily until she was forced to look away.

'When she had regained control of her voice, she began to lay down her rules. "Neither of you will ever set foot in this house again!"

'Finally Father spoke: "Margaret, I will not have my only child rendered homeless, like some common waif."

'"What of him?" she shouted.

'I spoke before Father could answer. "If Ryan leaves - I leave! Make no mistake, Father!"

'"You may both stay - for the moment," he replied.

'Mother hesitated: "Very well, your father shows you more mercy than I would have done of my own choice. But from this day until the day when you repent your mistake you will have access only to your bedchamber and the kitchen. You have disgraced this family and no longer deserve to be a part of it. As for you—" she gestured at Ryan, "you will have no more privileges in this house than the lowest servant. If you imagined that by disgracing our daughter you would become accepted into this family you are mistaken. Madeleine is but a foolish child, and after some time in your company, she will soon come to her senses." She looked to Father angrily, and he nodded his assent, regretfully.

'I had not thought it would be this awful. But, given time, I prayed that they would mellow. If they would only give Ryan a chance they could not possibly fail to change their minds about him.

'Ryan took my arm and we departed to the kitchen where our good Nancy waited with food and comfort. I hugged her tightly in thanks for the gift of my ring. Her cheeks turned pink with pleasure.

'"Never have I seen a pair so well-matched," she said, beaming, "You will be a credit to me."

[I break in here to remind you that I have already described Ryan and Madeleine's wedding night.]

'The next day, of all days to choose, Mr Pennington came to call. I had known that Mother had planned to give me to him in marriage but I had done nothing to encourage his belief in this matter. He was fifty years old, thirty-four years my senior, was of no interest to me and never had been. Mother knew this but had refused to accept it, that much was plain now. His carriage drew up outside and it sent her into a panic. She rushed upstairs to my bedchamber and, finding me alone, she began to threaten and bully me.

'"Come child," she said, dragging me by the arm, "we may yet save you from yourself. This ridiculous marriage can be annulled. By now I am sure you have realised your mistake." She glanced

123

meaningfully at the bed. "Mr Pennington need never know if we act quickly."

'"Mother, no!" I protested.

'"Do you—!' she shouted at me, "know what a fortune he is worth?'

'"I do not need his fortune," I responded, "and I most certainly do not need him - or any other man," and I too glanced meaningfully at the bed, a small smile curling my mouth. I admit, in retrospect, that this gesture may have been unwise, inflaming her still further as she grasped my meaning.

'"Harlot!" she shrieked. "Whore! See how he has already ruined you!"

'Before I could respond she glanced out of the window to see what the situation was below. I was surprised, and a little apprehensive myself, to see that Ryan was down there. He was standing with one foot planted firmly on the step of Mr Pennington's carriage thereby preventing that gentleman from alighting. Mr Pennington was blustering somewhat and I assumed from his countenance that he was threatening Ryan in some way. By now Mother had taken in the scene and she left in a rush.

'Meanwhile I saw Ryan lean forward and take hold of Mr Pennington by his collars. He said something, I know not what, and Mr Pennington subsided back into his seat. Ryan let go of him and signalled to the driver to move off. At this point Mother appeared on the steps, and at the sight of her Mr Pennington gestured and seemed to instruct his driver to whip the horses on. The carriage left the grounds almost at the gallop, dust streaming out behind it. Mother began to berate Ryan bitterly. I saw him turn on his heel and return inside, ignoring her.

'When he came back up to me, I asked him what had been said. He told me that Mr Pennington had been demanding to see me, refusing to believe I was married and calling Ryan a liar. Ryan had asked Mr Pennington if he should take this to be a challenge to a duel, and that had caused Mr Pennington's hasty departure.

'My relationship with my parents, particularly Mother, became only worse as time went by. I had foolishly believed that once Ryan was my husband they would accept our love, that they would see that there was nothing more they could do. I had truly feared for his safety before and had thought marrying him would keep him safe from harm. I kept hoping and praying that seeing how happy he made me would make them relent, but obviously my happiness meant little to them. I had never really comprehended Mother's truly malicious nature or the power she held over my father. She never let an opportunity pass if there were a chance of hurting or humiliating Ryan and, therefore, me as well. Any servants that showed us any sympathy were dismissed from service. At least we managed to keep Nancy, partly because she had been with the family for so long (and I think Father balked at the idea of dismissing her) and partly because we kept her support as secret as possible.'

❧

All through our journey the part of me that held Madeleine could not be stilled. I felt her all the time, egging me on like a cheerleader.

Well, we made it to Nashville and, despite having to drive on the 'wrong' side of the road, Tony got us safely to Goodlettsville which was about twenty miles from the airport. This was where we were staying. I was thinking all through the journey how lucky I was to have Tony by my side. Without him I would never have made it this far.

We were exhausted by the trip but I was all eyes, soaking up the atmosphere and not entirely convinced that I wouldn't spot Garth on the sidewalk or driving the other way. Every Stetson or baseball cap spelled the possibility.

⁂

Two days after Mr Pennington called at the house (and I never knew about this as Madeleine), Ryan approached Margaret in a way that must have cost him dearly. I never knew him to surrender his pride in this way at any other time. It makes me love him all the more that he did this, and I can only pray that he knew how much I did love him. You will, I am sure, have realised by now that even I am sometimes confused as to who I am! Please forgive me for this confusion. It seems to be a common problem with regressions.

He made sure that they would have some privacy, by waiting for Margaret as she returned to the house from the dairy after her routine visit there in the mid-morning. He stood concealed in the shadows of the barn, stepping out into the light as she approached. She took a step back, startled by his sudden appearance.

"What do you want?" she snapped.

Ryan raised his hands in a placating gesture, not wanting her to feel threatened, and answered her quietly: "Just a moment to speak with you."

126

She did not answer but merely folded her arms, impatience written across her countenance, so he continued, taking her silence for assent. "I know very well that I am not what you hoped for…"

"In no conceivable way!" she interrupted, glaring at him.

"I know - I know," he carried on. "You have made this very plain. But, believe me, I am not here to try to gain anything from you or Madeleine's father. I love Madeleine, surely you must allow this to count for something?"

"Love! - Love! What good is love? Love will not pay taxes! Love will not feed you! Oh, why did you come here? - she had every chance of a future—and now you have ruined everything for her!"

Ryan dropped his hands to his sides. He surrendered his eye contact with Margaret and stared down at the ground. He paused, gathering his thoughts, one boot stirring the dust underfoot.

He spoke again, quietly, he hoped persuasively, his eyes still downcast. "I cannot change who or what I am, and I cannot stop loving Madeleine. But it is done. We are married now and it would make things so much better for all of us if you could only accept this - I have no shame where she is concerned - if it will help I will abandon all pride. Please, tell me what you want of me, save leaving without her, and I will try to satisfy you and Edwin."

Margaret's eyes flashed angrily, and her voice lashed at him, "There are many things you could do but none would save you from my wrath! Only death would save you! Now get out of my path and take care never to stand in my way again lest I am tempted to send you into death's embrace myself!" She started to push past him but he stepped sideways, barring her way.

"Very well," he said, as he lifted his eyes to hers once more. "Treat me however you see fit. But I warn you, never harm my wife, for that would be a mistake. I too have a temper and it would not be controlled, should Madeleine be hurt in any way."

He stood aside now and let her pass but not before she had seen the dangerous possibilities that lay deep within his eyes. He felt her anger turn to fear for a moment as she passed him.

After that Margaret never missed a chance to use her malicious tongue against him. Here are two examples that I have remembered.

'This particular episode began when she made one of her rare appearances in the kitchen. She did not often come into our domain, and I wished she had not on this occasion. She fixed her gaze on Ryan and me as soon as she came in, and Ryan sighed resignedly as he recognised the signs of trouble. We were to be her targets for the day. Most of the time we tried to keep out of her way or ignore her taunts. We had learned that it never did any good to argue with her. She was one of those sorry people one cannot get through to; she had no higher side and could never be convinced that she was wrong on any point.

'Whenever anything had annoyed her, as it clearly had on this evening, she would choose a victim to vent her frustration or temper on. Unfortunately that person was often Ryan. She began immediately, by pulling his supper plate away from him as if to inspect the contents. Ryan merely stared back at her neutrally, showing no emotion.

'"I see that we are still feeding you more than you are worth," she sneered.

'He did not answer. With good fortune, she would soon tire of her game, and leave to seek out

128

more easily intimidated prey. She pushed the plate back angrily, causing it to slop onto the table. Ryan resumed eating but I did not.

'She pounced on this instantly. "Madeleine, do not waste good food, especially when it is good food neither you nor this good-for-nothing has done anything to earn!"

'I could never accept her attacks on Ryan quietly or for long and she knew this very well; on this occasion I succumbed to her taunts, saying in his defence, "My husband works very hard for you, harder than the other workers, who are paid more than he - and you know that is the truth."

'But there was only one real way to stop her and that was to leave. Ryan and I left our meal, got up, and went out of the kitchen by the back door. But her usual ambition in this regard was to goad Ryan himself into a response; as she had not succeeded in this she followed us out. We had gone to sit on the bench among the rose beds. She started once more, as usual, never addressing Ryan by name. I do not believe I ever heard her speak it.

'"There is still much work to do in the fields. I would have thought that you would have been ashamed to sit idly while others work. Have you no pride? (Ryan had been working that day since five a.m., and it was now seven in the evening.) What kind of weakling are you?" she asked him, this last sounding so ridiculous as Ryan stood up, towering over her as he did by a good eleven inches. She, determined to be difficult, stood in his path so that he could not pass.

'Ryan had two choices, either to push past her or to turn back and take a different route, but he did neither. He put his hands on her waist and lifted her bodily out of the way, putting her back down at the side of the pathway; then we both hurried past her.

'But then, as we tried to walk away, she pushed back past us, so that once more she turned to block Ryan. "Do not ever dare to touch me again!" she screamed, white with rage and indignation. She continued vengefully, "What kind of upbringing did you have that it allows you to behave so impudently? Your own mother and father must have been glad to be rid of you!" She immediately saw, though he tried to hide it, that her remarks had hit a sensitive nerve, and she continued mercilessly. "If you even had a father! For if your mother was like most Irish sluts - she probably never even knew who your father was!" Now she could see that she had really hurt him, and so she smiled, satisfied.

'Ryan went very still, his jaw line rigid. His eyes continued to regard her for several long seconds, their colour deep and dark.

'Finally, cutting each word off tightly, he said, "Do not judge others by your own behaviour. You, are not fit even to speak of my mother. She may not have enjoyed in all her life the riches that keep you for one month - but she had that which you long for, and yet will never be able to buy - she had dignity. And she was what you can never be, for all your wealth - she was a lady!" He turned and walked past me, left the gardens by the back route and headed towards the woods. I glared at her.

'"Why," I asked, "why are you so cruel?" I hurried after Ryan.

'I found him where I expected to, at the big oak tree. He had his back to me and was leaning with his hands braced against the trunk, both arms rigid and his head down. When I reached him I put my hands tentatively on his shoulders. I could feel what

130

I presumed was a deep anger quivering in him. He turned to me in a rush and gathered me into his arms before I could even register his expression. He held me fiercely and I gradually realised that he was still trembling, but not with anger - he was crying. I held him tightly. I had never been able to persuade him to tell me of his mother, but at least he felt able to turn to me in his grief for comfort. Ryan's arms were resting heavily across my shoulders but I stood firm under his weight until he stood up once more, his grief purged for the moment. He leaned back against the tree, slid down the trunk, and sat at the base, drawing me down to sit between his legs. I leaned back against him, the back of my head resting on his chest. He put his arms around me and I took his hands in mine, wrapping him around me like a cloak.

'"Do you wish to talk about your mother?" I asked gently.

'He did not answer for a few moments, then he said, almost in a whisper, "Only—" he swallowed, "only to say that I wish you had a mother like mine."

'I did not press him further for I could hear in his voice that to do so would have upset him again. So we just sat, drawing comfort from each other's closeness.'

❧

Here is yet another example of her vicious tongue, and her vindictiveness towards Ryan. This occurred seven months after the wedding.

'In the winter of 1638 several of the household and most of the workers were struck down with the ague [like influenza. This was a more serious

131

condition in those days, often fatal, and there were, of course, no paracetomols to reduce temperature]. This was a terrifying epidemic. Some of the farm labourers who had succumbed to the disease had lost their lives. I believe this was because of their poor, damp housing together with a lamentable lack of care. It made my blood run cold to think that had Ryan become ill during the winter before he came to me that he too may have died from lack of care and sustenance.

'I knew something was amiss as soon as I awoke, for the dawn was already breaking, slashing the sky with pink and amber, yet Ryan still lay asleep beside me. Under normal circumstances he would have awoken me as he left to go to his work at about five o' clock, while it was still dark. As it was he seemed to be deeply asleep. I touched his shoulder to rouse him and, to my horror, I found that his skin burned like a fiery coal. But he did, nonetheless, awaken at my touch. He was very thirsty so I fetched him some water. When I returned with it I was filled with dismay to find him fully clothed, apparently determined to go to his work. I stepped up close to him, placing a restraining hand on his chest. His very breath felt hot on my face, and I could feel the clammy heat radiating from him through his shirt. His eyes were glassy.

'"Ryan," I pleaded, "you cannot leave your bed. You are in no fit state to work."

'He took the water from me, and drained the cup. "It is all right. I was merely thirsty, that is all, and now I feel better. Besides, if I do not work, your parents are bound to hear of it."

'"I do not care if they hear of it. You need to stay here in the warm, not work outside. It is freezing this morning. Look at the ice on the glass." It was

132

true; the insides of the windows were coated with the frond-like patterns of frost, despite the fire burning in the grate.

'"I am a little tired, that is all," he insisted. "I promise, should I feel worse, I will return to you. But I must try. So many are sick that there are barely enough to milk the cows or tend the horses. I promise you I will return as soon as I can."

'Reluctantly I had to let him go. I could do little else as, even though he was ill, he was yet far stronger than I. However, I watched with grave misgivings from the back window as he crossed to the dairy. It seemed to me that his shoulders sagged dispiritedly and he gave a cough as the frigid air thread its icy fingers into his lungs. I could see how bitterly cold it was by the clouds of white that appeared as he breathed out and I could also see that his breathing was too rapid to be a sign of good health. He disappeared into the dairy and I decided to go down to the kitchen. There I discovered Nancy who was bustling around under stress of overwork. As I had feared, she told me that Ryan had refused any breakfast.

'I myself prepared him some hot soup which I would take out to him. But when I went to the dairy with it Ryan was not there. It appeared that word had come of a cow that had fallen into a ditch and become trapped. The cow was bogged down and in danger of drowning in the mud if it were not saved. The only two men available had been Ryan and one other, so they had gone with ropes to pull the cow out of the mud.

'They did save the cow but, when I saw them returning, the other man was supporting Ryan. I observed them coming from the kitchen window where I had been anxiously keeping a look out. The

133

moment I saw them I ran out in a panic and almost crashed to the rock-hard ground as I slipped on its treacherous surface. Ryan still had his senses and was trying to walk but he stumbled along unsteadily. I helped the other workman get Ryan upstairs where he collapsed onto the bed. His clothes were sodden and his skin was freezing. He shivered uncontrollably. The other man told me that they had succeeded in their efforts to pull the cow out of the ditch after a long, wet struggle against the elements, but that Ryan had grown steadily weaker throughout the morning, finally falling to the ground as the cow made off, unhurt. As he left the room, with a glance at the bed, the man crossed himself. I knew this meant two things. First, the man was thanking the Lord that he had been spared the sickness until now, and, second, that he believed Ryan would die. I would not allow it. I could not bear it.

'There was no-one on whom I could call for help, for those who were not already stricken themselves were exhausted from nursing those who were. I hurried over to the bed. Ryan's cheeks were flushed, and now, although he still shivered violently, his skin was hot through the wet clothes. I swiftly began to pull them off. It was difficult for Ryan was curled up tightly, trying to feel warm. But eventually I threw the last soaked item onto the soggy heap on the floor. I drew the blankets up around him, then I too climbed into the bed and wrapped my body around his, to try and warm him with my own heat. It was all I could do for I knew that fever victims must have the fever sweated out of them. [Of course today we know better.] Later I would go down and prepare him some herbal infusions that Nancy had shown me in the past.

'After a while Ryan stopped shaking with the cold and began to sweat. He tried to throw off the covers but I kept them pulled up tight to his neck. Later he seemed to sleep, so I got up and banked up the fire. By now it was afternoon and I lit every candle in the room, in an attempt to hold back the pervading gloom. This day, the coming twilight made me feel afraid, something I never usually felt if Ryan were with me. His face was wet with sweat while his hair was curled and damp with it. It glistened on his black eyebrows and ran in salty pearls down his cheeks. I dampened a rag in the wash basin and wiped his skin with it. By now the bedclothes were wet, and I was very afraid at the intensity of the heat pouring from his body. He became restless, constantly pushing at the covers, and he mumbled to himself, whispering names and words I did not understand. His eyes were still closed but he did not seem to be truly asleep - not peacefully in any event. I sat on the bed and cradled his head in my lap. He seemed to know I was there and he snuggled against me for comfort. I leaned down and gently brushed his lips with mine. They felt dry and fiery to the touch. I did not know what else to do for him. Then I remembered - the herbal infusion! I got down from the bed, and with an anxious glance back to where he lay, I went down to the kitchen and set to work.

'It took me a little over an hour to prepare the drink, and as soon as it was ready, I hurried back to him. He was not in the bed, I saw at once. In my concern I almost did not see him where he lay - in front of the fire. He was shivering uncontrollably again and had obviously crawled to the fire to try and get warm. He awoke at my presence and told me that his head was sorely paining him, that his throat felt raw and spiteful. I gave him the drink I

135

had prepared and he drank it gratefully, though he was barely able to hold the cup steady for the quaking of his body. The drink seemed to soothe him and he lay back down with a sigh. I fetched a blanket, and wrapped it around him, then I lay down with him once more to warm him.

'Suddenly, just at this moment, our bedchamber door flew open without even an enquiry or a knock, and Mother stormed into the room. I sprang to my feet, angered and shocked at her abrupt appearance in our domain.

'"What is it?" I demanded to know.

'"What is it!" she repeated. "The entire farm is falling into ruin, with so many confined to their sick beds, and I find him here with you, like this! And you ask - what is it!" She strode towards us, "You!" she pointed at Ryan. "You take too much advantage of our kindness to you! You spend time here with our daughter, teaching her your vile ways while others work!"

'"Mother!" I shouted to silence her, "Ryan is ill! He made his condition worse than it need have been, saving your stock from harm. Have you no compassion at all? Leave him be!"

'"So—" she said in a sneering tone, "still you hide behind a woman's skirts. Get up! Stand on your own two feet for once in your miserable existence!"

'I could see from the corner of my eye that Ryan was indeed getting to his feet, pulling himself up on shaky legs, and bracing himself against the fire wall.

'I turned back to him, "No, my love." The illness was confusing him so that he was allowing her to goad him. I put out a hand which he was forced to grasp for I could see that his head still spun with the fever. He could not stand for more than a

136

moment, and despite the support from my hand, he sagged against the wall, his legs betraying him. The rug began to slip from him and, to save him from this final humiliation, I clutched it quickly and wrapped it around him more securely.

'"Mother," I said coldly, "leave us now for I am sure we would not be welcome in your chambers."

'She did not like this thinly veiled reference to her and Father's private affairs, and so with a contemptuous toss of her head she left our bedchamber, slamming the door with all her might.

'Ryan collapsed back onto the rugs, with a pent-up breath rasping from him. He rubbed his hand wearily over his aching head. I held him, stroking his temples to try and ease the pain which was made worse by the fact that he still shuddered with chill. As soon as he slept once more I fetched fresh bed linen and remade the bed, so that I could help him into it for the night. Twice more he awoke in discomfort and the infusion, though cold by then, helped him back into healing sleep.

'I thanked the Lord that Ryan was so strong, for by morning his skin, whilst still too warm, was not so terrifyingly afire, and he had regained his full senses by that afternoon. He was then very anxious to rise from his bed but when he tried, despite my protests, he had to still admit best to the fever. He was too weak to walk but a few steps before dizziness overcame him, blackness swirling around his head.

'Ryan detested this physical weakness more than all the other unpleasant effects of this sickness. It seemed to me that since he had discovered at a very young age his own powerlessness against wealthy people he had relied on his considerable physical prowess to compensate him for this. Now he felt

137

helpless in every way and he could not stand it. He became angry with himself and pushed his body to the limit over and over again that day, striving to regain his strength. He was not satisfied until late into the evening when he was finally able to pace across the entire room.'

Chapter Fourteen

I had another memory on one of the planes, concerning Nancy.

Summer 1639 (fourteen months after the wedding)

'This was a time when Ryan was able to truly repay Nancy for all her kindness to us.

'He and I had been out for an early evening stroll and we were returning home by the longer route, using the lane. We heard the sound of a pony and trap approaching at a very fast pace and we stopped to see who it could be. When it hove into view we could see that it was Nancy who held the reins and that she was driving the pony on with a whip. When she saw us standing at the side of the road she pulled the pony to a sudden halt and climbed down to us, somewhat shakily. She was in an awful state and I had never seen her that way before.

'"Nancy, whatever is wrong?" I asked.

She took a faltering step towards Ryan, and he, sensing her need, put his arms around her.

'"It is all right Nancy," he said soothingly. She

began to cry, partly with relief I think, and I too put my arms around her. After a few moments, she became calmer.

'"Oh dear," she said, "such a dreadful business—" We waited: "Two men—villains, blackguards! They stopped the pony and demanded money or jewellery from me to let me pass. As if I look the part of a fine lady!"

'"What did they do to you?" Ryan asked anxiously.

'"They just frightened me half to death with vile threats and unseemly suggestions. I managed to drive the pony on through them. They chased me down the lane - Lord save us - they had knives!" She shuddered in remembered fear.

'Ryan tried to reassure her. "It is all right now. Get back into the trap. You too, Madeleine. I will follow on foot, lest they are still coming after you."

'"No!" I exclaimed. I would not hear of it. I was not going to leave Ryan to the mercy of two armed men, even if the trap was not meant to hold three. "You will ride with us, Ryan, or I will not leave." As it turned out it was fortunate for all of us that I did so insist for these turned out to be very determined brigands. Ryan could see from my expression that I would not be denied, so he rode standing on the back step of the trap, while Nancy and I rode inside.

We had been travelling for only a few minutes when two men, the same two men according to Nancy, came out of the woods just ahead of us and jumped down into the lane. They must have cut through the woods in order to catch us. I dread to think what might have happened had we come on alone and left Ryan far behind us. Nancy tried to drive the pony through them again but they had anticipated this and were carrying large leafy branches which they used to hit the pony about the head. Nancy tried to contain the frightened beast but he plunged from the road, rearing up at the bank, trying to climb it. Before anyone could prevent it, he had dragged the trap sideways up it. Then, still panicking, he galloped into the trees. I do not know how we were not all thrown off at this point, especially Ryan who clung to the back. But, after a few hundred paces, one wheel struck a tree and broke. Then we were all thrown out and the terrified pony turned for home, dragging the wrecked trap behind him.

'I rolled over and over, crashing through the undergrowth, thinking I would never stop, but finally I did, lying breathless for a moment. When I sat up I could see Ryan and Nancy in the same predicament. Ryan hurried over to me, and then to Nancy, to make sure we were unhurt. Fortunately we had landed in thick ferns which cushioned our tumble and we were unscathed. Once we were all on our feet, we began to make our way back to the lane. But then we could hear the two men coming - still they would not give up! They were making no attempt to move stealthily, and were obviously very confident. We backtracked quickly into the deeper woodland for we knew they had knives. We came across a dense thicket and crawled inside to hide.

'Nancy was terrified and she began to wail, "Lord save us! We shall be butchered!" She could not help herself but if she did not stop she would give our position away. Ryan placed a hand on each of her cheeks and turned her face until her eyes met his. "Listen to me, Nancy," he pleaded with her, "I swear I will not let them harm you! Nancy! Do you trust me - do you?"

'"Yes," she answered tearfully.

'He held her gaze to be sure that the hysteria had passed and repeated, "I will not let them harm you - I will die first - do you hear me?"

'"Yes," she responded again but in a steadier voice this time.

'Now the men were almost upon us. I cast about in my mind for a plan since it was obvious that they would find us in the end, and I did not want Ryan to try and tackle two armed men.

'He spoke again, "You must both trust me. I want you to come out of hiding - right away - before they find us at this disadvantage. Pretend you are alone but remember - you are not - and remember that I will not let them harm you."

'I looked into his eyes and, although I was deathly afraid of confronting these men, I did truly trust Ryan with my life. But I was also afraid for him. There being no time to argue or discuss, I grasped Nancy's hand and pulled her after me, out into the open. We did not need to feign fear, and we both clung to each other. I stifled a scream as the two men ran out of the trees and were upon us. At the sight of us they slid to a halt.

'"Well, well now," one said, "what do we have here? Ladies, do you not know it is foolish to venture into these woods so late in the day?" They seemed to anticipate no threat, and their knives at this point were sheathed in their belts. I began to hope that they had not in fact seen Ryan, crouched as he had been at the back of the trap, and that they thought us to be alone.

'"You are fortunate," one of the men said, "that it is we that have come across you, not some cut-throat robbers." He grinned, showing grimy, yellow teeth. He leered at his companion, and as their eyes

142

met, I needed no special powers to divine their intentions.

'"We will see that you are safe home, never fear," said the other, "after we have extracted a small payment." He too grinned in a revolting manner. "Come here!" he ordered, beckoning to me. I did not move.

'"I have nothing to pay you with," I replied.

'"Oh but you have, you have," he responded and, to my terror, he drew his blade, shouting at me, "Come here, now!" Still I did not move. The other man also pulled his knife.

'"Cut her!" he said. "Her appreciation of you will improve."

'My heart thudded in fear - *My god,* I thought, *he will really use it on me.*

'At that moment, to my surprise and relief, for I had seen no sign of his approach, Ryan suddenly stepped from behind a tree at their backs. He swung a hefty branch through the air, directed at the head of one of our would-be attackers. I truly do not know whether it was Nancy or myself who gave him away with a look of relief. But one of us did. The blow still landed and its power was still enough to fell the man, but he had turned and so the blow did not knock him senseless as it otherwise would have done. Ryan quickly struck again. This time the job was completed but the branch broke at this blow, and now the second man was warned. As the second blow fell on his companion he glanced at Nancy and me, and, knife in hand, he took a step towards us, his intentions clear.

'Ryan read this intention immediately, so he jumped over the fallen man and swiftly placed himself between us and the knifeman. The man advanced on him, his blade flashing from hand to hand as he sought an opening. Then he struck, the blade arcing through the air inches from Ryan's chest as my husband stepped back to avoid it. I could already imagine his blood spilling red against his white shirt and I whimpered in terror. Twice more the blade slashed through the air, and Ryan barely avoided it. Now he could retreat no more, for Nancy and I were close behind him, while behind us was an impenetrable tangle of bushes. My hands were against Ryan's back and there was nowhere left for us to go. Time seemed to slow down. I could feel his muscles through the rough fabric of his shirt, contracting as he drew back from the knife. I could feel his heart pounding with intense effort. And I could not bear it, for I could almost see him fall in front of me.

'Then suddenly it was over. Ryan saw the chance he had obviously been waiting for and grabbed at the man's knife. Immediately blood welled from Ryan's clenched fist, and I could see that his hand had not caught just the man's hand and the hilt but also part of the blade itself. The robber twisted the knife cruelly but Ryan would not let go. With his other hand he managed to deal the man a hefty blow to his ribs. The man fell and Ryan was able to wrest the knife from him. The man gasped for breath, Ryan quickly turned the knife and hit him hard on the temple with the heavy hilt.

'Only now that we were safe, did he clasp his injured hand and flinch at the pain. Nancy and I both took hold of his arm anxiously, and made him open the hand for us to see the extent of the wound. His palm was sliced across from one side to the other but the blade had turned, for, fortunately, it had cut broadly but not deeply. Nancy strode over to one of the fallen robbers, fearless now, and tore off a length of his shirt. This we used to bind Ryan's hand and staunch the bleeding. Then we both hugged him in thanks for saving us from these villains. I could see a new light in Nancy's eyes as she looked up at Ryan - she loved him too. Ryan may not have won the hearts of my parents but those who really knew him could not help but love him.

'We walked home in high spirits at our escape, arm in arm, the three of us.'

❧❧❧

The flights were particularly fertile as regards new memories, and this was another.

Twenty-seventh April 1639 (First wedding anniversary)

'It was a year to the day since Ryan and I were wed. I had wanted to find him a present to mark the occasion, something special and personal. I had no money because, since the day I had given myself to him, I had been denied any by my parents. However, Nancy helped me and together we made Ryan a new shirt from some fine dark blue cloth meant for a new gown. His only other two shirts were both a creamy white, and when he wore this blue one, his eyes took up its colour, enhancing their own until they were almost indigo.

'But my gift from him was a total surprise. I knew that he had been doing some extra work down in the village but I still cannot imagine how he managed it. He had a ring made for me from Welsh gold. It carried both our initials.

'I was totally speechless at first, but then I could not tell him enough times how much I loved him. It

145

was the most beautiful thing I had ever owned. But there was yet more to come. That evening, at twilight, we donned our cloaks and Ryan led me into the woods beyond the gardens. As we approached the small clearing in which stood our special tree, I could see strange lights twinkling through the branches. As we drew closer I caught my breath for I could see that the twinkling lights came from candles, dozens and dozens of candles, just as in the church on our wedding day. Ryan had put them on the branches all around the clearing.

'He had also laid a fire which he now lit, and we sat on rugs from the house, sipping wine and staring into the flickering light. I was completely captivated by this atmosphere. Ryan has never ceased to amaze me with the lengths he is prepared to go to in order to please me. It was at this time that I chose to ask him a thing which had begun to vex me. An older woman from the village had said to me a few days since that I could not continue to expect fidelity from him; that I should be ready to forgive him, should he stray, for he must be tired of just the one partner by now, as any man would be.

'So as we sat close together in the warmth of the fire, I said, "I know you have bedded others before me. How shall you compare me? Do I still satisfy you or do you regret being tied to me by wedlock? Are there sometimes thoughts of another you would prefer?" I held my breath for, though I was sure the woman was wrong, I loved him so much that the thought of losing him did oft cross my mind, and I was in need of reassurance.

'Ryan leaned towards me and kissed my lips softly, then he replied, 'It is true, you were not my first but you will be my last. There have been others in my life—' he paused; '—and they will always be remembered with affection by me, but they were before Madeleine, and since Madeleine I will never need another. You are truly everything a man could desire but, more importantly, I love you, and only you." Then he stunned me by saying, "And what of you and your pleasure? Are you content with this one man?"

'I answered him, "I have no-one to compare you with but I cannot conceive of attaining any greater pleasure than that which you give me. I will never accept any other but you as long as I live. You are my one love."

'At this affirmation of love and happiness, we lay down in the magical light.'

During the last flight, between Detroit and Nashville I had another recollection that was especially vivid because I presume we were drawing closer. And when, knowing what I did, I wished that Ryan had not been so gallant. Had he not helped Madeleine's stepmother this day, she might have died and then Ryan would have lived.

May 1640 (two weeks before the abduction)

'It was unlike Mother to go out alone but on this occasion she had. She had gone to collect flowers to lay out for some guests who were to arrive later. Normally she would have sent a maid out on this errand, but the whole household was busy preparing for her influential visitors.

'A storm broke, so suddenly that she had no time to get home before it was upon her in its full throes. She had always lived in dread of storms. They gave her the vapours from fear, even when she was safe indoors; but now she was outdoors, and alone, and her mind almost slipped from her in her panic. She could only cower in abject terror beneath a large oak tree, trying to shelter from the heavenly display of fire and destruction. She clung to the strength of the tree's massive trunk, eyes shut fast, whimpering in fear, and wet through.

'The thunder was indeed quite the loudest I had ever heard. Bolts crashed to earth with ear-splitting cracks, the very air quivering with the force of them. Father too was panic-stricken at the thought of her out there alone, and he shouted that all the men must go out and search for her. He feared that she would die, if not from a lightening strike then from sheer fright. Every available man was sent, including Ryan of course. She had never done anything to encourage him to help her, and he could have been forgiven had he refused to look for her. But his character would not permit him to turn his back on any creature in anguish, however evil that creature might be, so he went out. I did not try to stop him, for over the last two weeks she had found nothing malicious to say to him or me, and I had a tiny spark of hope growing in my heart that at last Ryan was beginning to win her over. [Little did Madeleine know that the only reason for this fragile peace was that the plans for Ryan's abduction had been completed, so Margaret was content that she would soon be rid of him.]

'The storm raged on, the vast amount of rain falling causing rivulets of water to run through the gardens, cascade down the steps, and wash across the driveway. I looked on from our bedchamber's back window but the sky was so dark that the only time I could see anything was when a lightening

148

flash split the gloom and lit everything up briefly. The men had been gone for thirty minutes, yet still there was no sign of any of them, or her.

'They had parted company in order to cover more ground, and Ryan was searching the meadow and the woodland above it. He almost missed her in the darkness. She could not be heard above the violence of the storm though she was screaming and crying. The thunder cracks were tearing the air continuously, accompanied by non-stop lightening flares.

'As Ryan pushed his way through the sodden branches, a tree to one side of him was struck by a bolt, and it split in two with an horrendous crash which shook the ground on which he stood. The tree disintegrated in a brief fireball which was followed by a sudden eerie moment of silence. Into this silence came a dreadful shriek of mortal fear from nearby. He tried to pinpoint it but the storm burst forth its power once more, deafening him.

'However, with the next brilliant flash the trees all around were lit up as if they were etched in silver, and he could see her where she crouched at the base of a massive tree. When darkness hit once more it was like deepest night after the violent light, and so, blinded, he had to progress towards her a few steps each time the sky lit up. When he was close enough he crouched next to her and put a hand on each of her trembling shoulders. There was no use trying to speak against the fury of the storm. She did not even realise who it was, but she turned into his arms instinctively with a sob of relief. She clutched fiercely at him, clawing at his back, almost insane with fear by then. He gathered her close to the shelter of his body, both to warm and calm her. She was shivering with cold and terror in equal measures. Then she looked up and saw his face clearly, and she realised whom she was nestled against. But her crazed mind refused to allow her to surrender her fear and replace it with her usual loathing, so this triumphant fear made her stay where she felt safe, in Ryan's arms.

'Gradually his strong presence stilled her hysterical sobbing, and she clung to him, somewhat soothed. They remained this way, her face buried in his shoulder, eyes shut tight to hide the onslaught from her sight, until finally, with a last reverberating crash, the storm ceased as rapidly as it had started. But still she seemed unable to move. So, as the downpour eased, and knowing that my father was distraught, Ryan drew her to her feet, and steered her towards home. Her trembling legs were as yet unable to support her, so he was still holding her close when they emerged from the woodland.

'Just as suddenly as the fickle sun broke through the sooty clouds, so her composure returned, and watching from the window, I saw a transformation take place. She drew herself upright and pushed Ryan's supporting arms away from her as if he were an attacker rather than her saviour. She looked disdainfully down her nose at him for a moment and then strode ahead of him into the house.

'Ryan paused, and looked up as if he knew I would be watching. He lifted his hands to me, palm up, in a gesture that said, "What more do I have to do to earn her approval?" Then he dropped them back to his sides, and walked into the house. When I had first seen that Ryan was the one to bring her safe home I had felt the spark of hope grow. Surely now she would see him in his true light but it seemed there was no end to her bitterness. Perhaps it made her even more resentful of him - that he had seen her weakness, and that she had needed to rely on him in her vulnerability. In any case not one word of gratitude ever passed her lips.

'When he came back into the bedchamber, Ryan's wet clothes clung to him like a second skin. The rain had been so torrential that it had soaked right through the heavy cloak he had worn. He came but a few steps into the room, then stood still, his head slightly bowed as if in deep and sad contemplation. He did not often admit to feeling hurt by her despicable behaviour but I think that, like me, he had harboured hopes that finally there might be a reconciliation. After a few moments he looked up at me, his eyes showing his deep disappointment, then, with a heavy sigh, he pressed his lips firmly together and shook his head slowly in total mystification.

'Despite the day returning to its normal heat, he was very chilled, so I drew him over to the fire, and he sat down on the rugs. He made no move to take off his wet clothes and after a while they began to steam in the heat from the fire. He sat staring into the flames, his elbows propped on his knees, cupping his chin in his hands. I sat down and leaned against him, trying to lift his spirits.

'Finally he spoke, "What have I ever done to her to make her hate me so?" he asked.

'I had no answer for him, so I put my hand to the back of his neck and entwined my fingers in his hair. He sighed again and lay down with his head in my lap. We sat this way, with me cradling him in my arms, and stroking his hair. We both knew in our hearts that nothing we could ever do would pacify her unhappy soul.

It seemed impossible, I think, to both of us that she could have clung so desperately to Ryan for comfort and support, the way she had been doing when they emerged from the woods, yet turn against him the way she had done when she no longer needed that physical comfort.'

We paid a visit to GB Management's offices while we were in Nashville. I had spoken to a very nice lady called Joan Cook on the telephone before we went to America. I had sent her some of this story and she had really liked it. She had also invited us to call in to meet her in person. Interestingly, she told me that she knew Garth very well, and that my portrayal of Ryan was so like Garth that she believed the story was true. It was great to walk where Garth had walked, and we also saw the chair in front of the fireplace where Garth had sat and been filmed accepting his Great British Country Award. We saw all his Gold and Platinum Discs and awards. Joan was very nice to us but she wasn't going to give away any secrets. She did tell us one funny story though. She said that when Garth had arrived to be filmed receiving his award, he had been wearing overalls because he had come straight from working on his tractor! Apparently, he had just rolled them down to his waist to reveal a T-shirt underneath, and was only shot from the waist up. That sounds so typical of the man I remember.

We stayed as long as we could without wearing out our welcome. I had of course hoped that Garth would just happen by. Joan had at least told us that he was in town. But finally we set off back to our motel. After we had rested for a while I began to get restless. I had yet another request to ask Tony. I wanted to try and find the home of Garth and his family. Amazingly we had flown over it on our approach to Nashville airport and I had been looking down at that precise moment. This would in no way help us find it on the ground though. I didn't want to intrude on them, but I suppose I was curious to see if I could find it; I also wanted to feel the atmosphere that surrounded his *real* life, as opposed to his show business one.

It was a weird experience. I knew that the location of the house was a well-kept secret in Nashville. And even the tour companies who did drive-bys of all the other stars' homes could not tell me where it was. I had nurtured a small hope that Joan in his office might be tempted to tell me, for she had been very kind when I had spoken to her on the telephone from England. But of course she could not. She was obviously tremendously fond of Garth and his family, and all her loyalty, quite rightly so, lay with them. So it was down to instinct, and crystals. I knew it was in a fairly remote spot, and that it lay somewhere in the vicinity of Goodlettsville. I had discovered this by dowsing over a map. But its exact location was something else again. I was able to direct us left and right etc., though as it turned out we did take a very roundabout route to it. We had travelled about eight miles off the main highway, and we were growing a little concerned, as we were running low on petrol. We seemed to be in the middle of nowhere and, after all, we were in a foreign country.

Then we turned a corner and there was a gas station. We called in and got fuel, then asked if they knew where the house was. The attendant told us we were just around the corner from it. Brilliant! They also told us that Garth himself often came into the garage for parts for his tractor! We followed his directions, drove up a rise, and there it was. Just as I had visualised, there were tall black wrought iron gates and red brick pillars at the entrance. The driveway disappears around a curve and trees hide the house from view. There is of course a security camera, and you have to enter a code into a computer keyboard to gain entrance. We could see three of the most beautiful quarter horses I have ever seen, grazing behind the fence. Their coats looked like pure silk.

We parked the car a few hundred feet from the gate, not having the nerve to park right up close, although there were already two other cars there, both containing fans. We stayed separate from them at first, because I wanted to soak up the feeling of his reality - and I did.

It is wonderful up there, the air smells so clean and sweet. I was more than satisfied at his home environment, and very happy that he lives in such a great place. I felt a great sense of peace and tranquillity sweep over me as I bathed in the nearness of this reality. But there was more to come. We chatted to the fans who were very friendly (we never met an American who wasn't!); in fact we became so friendly with another couple, Kim and Jeremy, that we still write to them to this day. I was told a story by the other lady who was there that filled me with joy and hope. She told us, for one thing, that Garth always comes out to speak to fans if he is there. She told us that he is totally natural with them, and has none of the airs and graces one might expect from such a big star, that she had the photos to prove it. She also showed us a photo of him with her daughter. The daughter looked like the shy type, and apparently had been very lacking in self-confidence at the time of the photograph. Her mother told us that Garth spent over an hour talking to her one day, showing her such respect and understanding that it changed her whole attitude to herself. This of course proved to me that Garth still has an awful lot of Ryan in his make-up.

After a while we all got very excited because we could hear a car approaching down the driveway. Panic almost set in, as we all tried to find the best place to stand. It wasn't Garth but it was Sandy, his wife. We couldn't believe it. She drove out through the automatic gates, which had opened on her approach and then, to our amazement, she stopped her car and rolled down the window to talk to us. I have to say that she is one of the sweetest and most genuine people I have ever met. She was so friendly and kind to us, especially when we spoke, and from our accents she realised how far we had come. She explained that, although Garth had been home, he had since left to go to Los Angeles She even let us take pictures of ourselves with her. It was quite funny, because just as I was trying to think of something to say or do to make us memorable to her should we ever meet again, Tony, who had been backing up a bank to get a better photo, slipped and then slid all the way down on his backside. We all laughed. Later I said to Tony that it was a brilliant move, that maybe Garth's wife would tell him about it and they would both remember us. She is so beautiful and she has the prettiest smile. And she smiles very readily, lifting your heart. It was wonderful to know that 'Ryan' is with such a great partner in this life and that he is in such safe and caring hands. For it is obvious, by the way she speaks about her husband, that she adores him.

One slightly disturbing realisation to come out of this meeting, though, was that when we first heard the car coming we naturally imagined that it might be Garth himself; as the car drew near it really hit me for the first time that 'Ryan' could be in the car. I had been so busy trying to meet the mega-star that I hadn't really realised how I would react on seeing Ryan again. I knew that it would be very emotional, of course, but until that moment I hadn't realised quite how traumatic it would be. How was I going to feel if it really happened? Meeting Garth Brooks was one thing, meeting Ryan would be something else! The chances of my keeping my cool if we did meet were starting to look very remote!

It has crossed my mind many times that I may have a better chance of getting to know Garth if and when he takes a back seat in the music business. Maybe then he won't be so heavily defended and I might be able to get closer. For my wanting to know him has nothing to do with his fame. But I can't imagine his vast army of fans letting him do that for quite a while.

Chapter Fifteen

That night I had a new insight - not surprisingly. It seems fairly appropriate that it should have come at this time, for it involves a time when Ryan was searching desperately for Madeleine who had mysteriously disappeared. I feel a little desperate myself sometimes, in my quest for contact with Garth, for he seems to be equally elusive.

1639 (about a year after the wedding)

Ryan bent his knees and hunkered down, rubbing his hands over his face, feeling the dampness of the sweat beaded there. He did not know where to look next. Where could she be? He felt fear tugging at him, cold and unwelcome. He swallowed. *Oh God*, he thought, *why does it have to be this way?* His very skin tingled with sick apprehension. This was not a fear he could stand and face, fight if necessary. All he could do was to continue to search, in increasing torment.

He thought back to two days ago when it had all started. It had been bedtime, and he tried to glean some clue from what had happened, to help him discover Madeleine's present whereabouts. She had been summoned to the drawing room and he had waited anxiously for her return, listening closely for any sound of trouble. By the time she had returned to the bedchamber she had seemed tired and uncommunicative. Ryan was in bed by then and he drew her in beside him, skin against skin. She had not wanted to talk, only to sleep. He had been undemanding, and merely cradled her to him comfortingly.

The next morning all seemed normal, and Ryan and Nancy were sent into Southampton early on a regular errand. But when they returned, in the early evening, they were greeted at the gate by several armed men. Nancy was allowed to continue inside, but Ryan was forced at sword point to get down from the cart, and he was not permitted any further.

Nancy was distraught and had protested but there was nothing she could do, only to call out to Ryan, 'Do not leave! Wait for me!'

Leave? That was the last thing he was thinking of. He did not know what to do though. His mind reeled in confusion, screaming out, wanting to know what was happening. But he had no-one to turn to. He sat down at the side of the gate, despite the threats of the armed men, and made it plain by his demeanour that he was not leaving. Finally, as darkness began to creep across the landscape, shadows running before it, Madeleine's mother and father walked haughtily down to him. Ryan stood up. Madeleine's father tossed a pouch of coins at him. He made no move to catch it and the bag bounced off his chest, and fell to the ground.

'Your bribery will not work now,' he said, somewhat perplexed, 'as it did not work before.'

'This is not a bribe,' her father told him, 'It is more…compensation. Madeleine has finally seen the error of marrying below her station. She is in her bedchamber, and she will not leave it until you have left the county.'

'No,' Ryan responded, no doubt in his voice. 'What you say is impossible.'

'Are you so vain?' Margaret asked archly. 'Did you not realise that this would happen sooner or later? Your boorish ways were bound to offend her in the end. What do you think we were discussing with her last evening?'

Ryan could not answer for he did not know. But he had unshakeable belief that they were lying. Madeleine simply would not - could not do this to him.

'I will tell you,' Margaret continued, smiling, for she realised that he indeed did not know what they had discussed. 'She told us that she had tired of your common ways. But she was afraid to tell you herself, for fear that you would strike out at her as you have at others when they have angered you.'

Ryan's eyes narrowed. He had not doubted Madeleine but, had he done so, this statement would have proved the falsehood.

So now he could answer, 'You tell a poor lie. Madeleine knows one thing above all others. She knows that I would never hurt her. You have tried to be too clever, and your plot has floundered.'

'Believe what you will. Madeleine will not see you again. She will not leave the house, and if you are wise, you will not try to enter it.' With this her father turned to the armed men. 'See to it that he leaves. If necessary—run him through!' (No doubt if Ryan had been put to death that night, Madeleine's parents would have tried to convince *her* that *he* had

159

left of his own accord. She would not have believed them.)

Ryan turned away in disgust, leaving the money pouch where it lay. He looked back over his shoulder to see Margaret stoop to retrieve it, and then he entered the woodland. Once he was out of sight and could no longer feel their cold gaze between his shoulder blades, he climbed up into a tree to think. He knew they were lying about Madeleine being in the house. If she were - then she would never have allowed this to happen. He sighed heavily. If he knew what he had to do to win Margaret and Edwin over, then he would do it. But it had gone too far. Margaret's hatred of him was obsessive.

He knew another thing for sure; he was not going to leave, nothing would make him do that. With Madeleine he had found a life - and love. It was hard, very hard at times, to withstand the constant bombardment of hatred that was directed at him but his life without her now would be meaningless. Whenever the two of them were together it made up for all the tough times. She healed him and he knew she felt the same.

He slid down from the tree and made his way through the woods, so that he would be able to see the main gate and yet remain unobserved. He put a hand to his stomach to stifle the sound as it rumbled loudly - he was hungry but that would have to wait. Darkness overtook the land, yet there was a bright full moon flooding the earth with her white power. Madeleine did not come home that night. He grew very concerned. Where was she? He would not contemplate that her parents were telling the truth. For one thing it could not be withstood, and anyway he knew Madeleine as well as he knew himself. She loved him with her whole being and she would never be parted from him voluntarily. That was his real worry because she must therefore surely be hidden somewhere, a prisoner. He hated not knowing her whereabouts. He spent a fairly uncomfortable night, growing hunger adding to his woes. He had been able to drink from the brook so he thanked God that at least thirst was not a problem.

Thankfully also, Nancy did not let him down. The first tendrils of early morning light had barely begun to creep against his eyelids when he heard her calling out to him. He responded, rubbing sleep from his eyes. 'Nancy? I am here.'

She appeared through the trees and he almost ran to her, for here he knew was comfort. He hugged her in appreciation of her loyalty and she hugged him in return.

'Thank the Lord,' she breathed fervently. 'Madeleine would never have forgiven me if you had left. Here—' she handed him a cloth containing bread and cheese.

'Nancy, you are a true and treasured friend, thank you. But - have you seen her? Do you know where she is?' Ryan asked, hoping against hope that she could give him a positive answer.

'I can only tell you that she is not in the house,' she responded, disappointingly. She placed a consoling hand on his arm, 'Ryan, I wish I could tell you more. But I can only tell you that Madeleine loves you, and she cannot be a party to what is happening here.'

'Thank you Nancy, but that is something I do not fear. I just—I cannot—' he paused, suddenly finding it hard to speak; 'I cannot stand not knowing where she is.'

Nancy was sorely troubled, *Why?*, she thought, *Why is it that when these two have only one wish - to be together - why can the rest of the world not leave them in peace?* This constant persecution of these two souls, was a never-ending source of horror to her.

That had been two days ago, and ever since, Ryan had been searching all the buildings on the estate, and the neighbouring ones, convinced that Madeleine must be a prisoner. But he had found no trace. Now he was exhausted. She was not in the near vicinity, of this he was sure. They must have taken her miles away - how would he ever find her? He contemplated storming the house, and forcing them to tell him the truth. He had seen this morning that her parents had removed the armed guards, just because he had disappeared from their immediate sight. It seemed that they really believed he had gone. This stunned him. Did they really think his love to be so shallow? That he would give up so quickly? Obviously they did, and it saddened him to think that they still did not understand. He and Madeleine were two halves of the same thing, and could not survive apart.

By now his hands and arms had been scratched and torn by brambles, from when he had searched the remote overgrown reaches of the farm - disused barns that may have held a secret prisoner. He was dirty and tired. His limbs ached from the ground he had covered. But most of all it was his heart that ached.

Two hours later he found himself walking along the main road. He had been drawn there by some unknown force that he was too tired to resist. When the carriage appeared, he thought he must be dreaming. For seated up next to the driver, typically, was Madeleine. She cried out when she saw him, obviously delighted at this unexpected rendezvous. Ryan's energy reappeared, as if by magic, and he ran towards the carriage, his heart thumping in his chest. The carriage pulled up sharply, the driver having no choice, for Ryan all but threw himself under the horses' hooves. Madeleine half-climbed, half-fell from the tall seat, for she could see that something was amiss. Ryan caught her, lifted her, and spun her around, before setting her back on her feet and kissing her soundly, his eyes glistening with released joy.

'What is it? What is it?' she gasped, breathless from the kiss.

Ryan was almost speechless, but he managed to ask, 'Where have you been?'

'Did you not get my message?" she asked puzzled, 'I left it for you in our bedchamber.'

'I have been denied access to the house, or even the grounds, since my return from Southampton.'

'You have—what?—oh my God!' Now she understood, and she tightened her embrace, horrified at what he must have been through. 'I have only been at my aunt's. She has been dying these past days, and she had asked for me to attend her.'

'Your parents,' Ryan explained, 'told me that you were in the house but that you had tired of me. That you were afraid to face me, for fear that I would hurt you.'

'You did not—?' she broke in but Ryan held up a hand in denial.

'No. I did not believe them. But—' He stopped for a moment, staring intently at her face, then he closed his eyes and sighed, the tension only now beginning to release him. 'I did not know where you had gone. I have been searching—searching every place I could think of. I feared you were a prisoner and I could not find you—I could not find you!' This last exploding from him on a sobbing breath of emotion. Madeleine realised now the extent of his distress. She took in his eyes bruised from lack of sleep, his mouth drawn with worry, the stained and ragged look of his clothes, and the blood on his hands and arms.

'My God,' she said. 'Oh Ryan—' Now she hugged him wordlessly, her body speaking for her the words she could not find with her voice. After a while they both climbed into the carriage. Madeleine wanted to confront her parents, to rail and scream at them for their cruel behaviour. But Ryan persuaded her that the best way to make them see that they were wrong and had failed was for the two of them to return home together, reunited as if nothing had happened. As they rode, Madeleine solved the rest of the mystery for him. When she had been summoned to the drawing room the night before she disappeared, it was merely to face one more set of demands to admit that their marriage had been a mistake which of course she had refused to do. The verbal attack on her and Ryan had left her weary, and she had seen no point in troubling him with an account of it. The call to her ailing aunt the next morning had just been an opportune coincidence which her parents had taken full advantage of.

Ryan had been right in that they should quietly return home together. Margaret's face when they strolled in, arm in arm, was sweet revenge. She was devastated.

❧❧❧

When the time came to leave America, I was a little tearful to be leaving not only a great country, with wonderful people who had made us feel at home, but of course to be leaving Garth as well, especially as my quest to meet him was still unfulfilled. But at least I had seen where he lived, met his wife, and seen his offices.

It was quite strange to come home again, but lovely to see all of our animals fit and well. I always worry so when I have to leave them. I took up riding my young horse again and the weather stayed good into November. I was still churning out songs and getting a little higher up the ladder with each one that was successful.

The good news was that I finally got tickets for a concert in Dublin the following May. Although it did mean another wait.

After we had been home a while I began to wonder what had happened to Madeleine. She was very quiet in my mind. Perhaps we had completely melded back together now. But anyway I knew the truth, and I had satisfied her by making an official record of the events of their lives. Maybe I didn't need to know any more. Now I had to pick up my life and move on. My relationship with Tony had only grown stronger through all my discoveries, and I loved him more than ever for helping me so much. I had also been bitten by the travel bug, and I was keen to start a new adventure. With royalties starting to come in from my songs, we were in a better financial position to take more holidays.

However, Madeleine's influence did return eventually.

Chapter Sixteen

Finally I got the last part of the puzzle. This is how Ryan and Madeleine fell in love.

'Ryan fascinated me totally from that first day when he had saved me from being assaulted. I spent as much time as possible talking to him or simply watching him at his work. And, for his part, he seemed happy enough to have me there. When it became obvious to my parents that I would not let them send him away, they grudgingly agreed to give him some work in the fields and allowed him to sleep in the barn, thinking that I would soon tire of him. He was not paid but was given all the food he could eat, and he seemed content with this. I had not been happy of recent years. My natural mother, Rebecca, had died when I was but six years old. Despite my young age, Father had allowed me to become the lady of the house in order to ease my grief. We had slowly been making a new life without Mother but then Margaret had come into our lives. Father married her without giving me any warning, and she had been introduced to me as his new wife, and my new mother. I had seen through my young and knowing eyes that she did not love Father. She was much younger than him and had married him, I was sure, merely to improve her station in life. [This may have been the reason why she expected Madeleine to marry for the same reasons, and had not understood when she would not. I think too that Margaret may have become very jealous when she saw Ryan and Madeleine's kind of love, for it was something she knew she would never have herself.] Father was besotted with her, and four years later he agreed to her demand that we should move to a grander house. In this way, I felt that she had taken my childhood dreams from me. She and I were never compatible, her ambitions and mine being so completely different.

'By the time I had reached the age of twelve it was obvious that Margaret had her own plans for me. Father had by now insisted that I call her Mother, though it grieved me to do so. She announced to Father and I that I was to marry a city gentleman. This, I realised, was but to enhance the family name further, and as the gentleman in question was some thirty-odd years my senior, the obvious intention was that I would soon add his fortune to the family coffers. I certainly had no intention of being wed to this old man, and I had left her in no doubt of it.

'We lived in an uneasy truce until two years later when Ryan came along. And, as she began to sense a growing closeness between us, she must have been concerned that her plans were going awry. She tried to turn my attention to other things, keeping me in the house as much as she could. She dare not forbid me to see Ryan or send him away, for she knew I would not tolerate it and, indeed, had she done so, it would have drawn me to him more tightly. I could never keep my mind on lady-like things for very long, and each time she left me I soon escaped and sought Ryan out. I was not happy unless I was with him. I began to feel uneasy unless he was close by. When we parted at night-time I could hardly sleep for wanting the morning to come sooner, so that I could be with him once more. Mother became more desperate and tried to distract me through other young men - young men from 'good' families whom she knew she could control, unlike Ryan.

'But all the time they talked to me their talk was merely of hunting and the excellence of their prospects. They bored me so. And I could only compare them to Ryan who talked to me of the meaning of life, of deep inner feelings, and not of the trivial subjects that the others thought of interest. I began to notice strong feelings of physical attraction too for the first time in my life. I'm sure the other ladies would have been shocked at my thoughts, impure as they were. Ryan's physique is powerful. He is tall, taller than all the other workers. [The average height in the seventeenth century was considerably less than it is today, and therefore Ryan, nearing six feet, was very tall.] He has wide shoulders and strong arms and legs. I have often seen him move a load that was beyond the others, yet his broad hands are capable of such gentleness. His brawny build makes it easy for him to intimidate other men and, coupled with his strong character, this makes me feel very well protected when I am with him.

Having said this, he is a very even-tempered man, except in cases of injustice, when his mood can be fiery. Ryan's facial features are very pleasing to me. He has black hair and cornflower blue eyes which make his colouring striking. He has a straight nose, not hooked like my father's, and his lips are full and inviting. He has a clear and even complexion, not marked and scarred like so many others. He also has the most exquisitely shaped ears, something most people would not notice, but I notice everything about him. When he smiles his face changes in an instant from a somewhat severely handsome countenance to one that elicits strong maternal feelings in kindly souls such as Nancy. For myself, I can say that the emotions he elicits from me are not in the least part maternal.

'After Ryan had been with us for a while, my mind would turn to wild imaginings. I began to wonder what it would be like to have those strong arms around me, to feel his powerful body pressed against mine, and, most of all, how it would feel to be kissed by that extravagant mouth. I began to look for excuses to touch his hand or rest my hand on his shoulder. More than once while out walking, I confess, I pretended to stumble in order to have him steady me with his hand. Ryan was always circumspect with me, indeed I began to think that I held no allure for him. But his eyes could not lie, and I could see it writ there as plain as day. He did care for me, I knew this to be the truth. I did not understand why he held back so.

'It was Nancy who finally explained to me that Ryan would never approach me romantically. He had of course been warned from doing so by Mother and Father, but that alone would not have stopped him - at least I do not think so. More than that, Nancy explained, he did not, and would never, consider himself a suitable prospect for me. It was most frustrating. How could I make him see that there was no other I would rather have?

One warm late summer night, [this must have been in 1637] as I lay alone in my bed, almost fifteen years old and ready to become a woman, I lay awake,

169

thinking only of Ryan. I imagined him also lying, unable to sleep for thoughts of me, in his bed of straw out in the barn. I pictured myself boldly approaching him, silhouetted in the moonlight, the shape of my body outlined beneath my thin night-gown. I imagined Ryan, overcome with desire for me, leaping to his feet, lifting me in his arms, and then laying me down in the straw. I saw us kissing fervently but then my mind could go no further for I was totally unknowing of the ways of the flesh. My dream collapsed and I drifted to sleep.

'The very next night, grasping my courage with both hands, I decided to act. (I was partly afraid of what might become of me when alone with a man for the first time, should he desire me, partly afraid of being rejected by him.) I wrapped a dressing gown around myself, over my night-gown, and made my way secretly downstairs and out to the barn doors. One was ajar and I peeped fearfully around it. I could see him curled up asleep in the straw, a rug pulled half across him. I crept inside and over to where he lay. Perhaps I would just look on him for a while, and then make my way back to bed.

He looked very appealing to me in his repose. He was lying on his back, one hand cradling his head, while the other lay relaxed on the straw. His face was smooth in sleep and his dark lashes lay soft against his cheeks. The rug covered him to his chest, a few dark wisps of hair showing over its edge. It appeared that he might actually be naked under the rug for I knew that he possessed no nightwear, and only a single shirt and breeches. I watched the soft rise and fall of his chest as he slept, hardly able to believe my own daring, almost feeling in my apprehension as if I were standing next to a sleeping tiger. I sat down and just watched him for a few minutes. Then it was no longer enough. His black hair was released from its queue and lay in disarray around his head. I reached out and touched it with a feather-like gentleness. He did not stir. I grew bolder yet and softly trailed a fingertip across the palm of his upturned hand. Still he did not move. I began to suspect that perhaps he had been awake since I entered, and was feigning sleep until I should tire and leave. I reached up to touch his cheek and, as my fingers were about to brush his skin, his eyes flicked open and he regarded me solemnly. I gasped - I was mortified, and I was ready to flee. Then he smiled. It was truly like the sun emerging from behind a cloud. My returning smile was without volition on my part and we regarded each other silently for a few heartbeats.

'But then, without warning, he reached up with a hand, and placing it firmly behind my head, he pulled me down to him, so that my body fell onto his.

'"I have longed to love you," he whispered.

'Our lips met and my mouth melted into his. I had been right, his mouth was made for kissing. The skin of his chest was hot against my hands which were pinned beneath me. This fire coursed right through my body, shocking me. I had never felt anything like this before.

'I became afraid of this loss of control, and I tried to pull back, but he held me firm against him. I struggled for a few seconds and then subsided, letting my body mould to his. If I was meant to drown this way - then let me drown. He could at that point have made any use of me that he wished, but in the end it was he who pulled away. He pushed himself up into a sitting position, careful to take his rug with him. He seemed unable to meet my eyes.

'"Forgive me," he murmured quietly.

'"But," I protested, "it was my own doing. I came upon you in sleep." From what I had been told of men he was bound to have reacted in that manner, and, I had expected, much worse.

'"No," he said, "you do not understand. Madeleine—" I could see that he was thinking quickly, trying to find a way to undo what he had done. He continued: "I did not realise that it was you." I was certain this was not true. He had looked directly into my eyes, and there was bright moonlight flooding in through the open door. But before I could break in he said, "It is impossible - I cannot love you - no-one would allow it."

'"I care not for anyone else," I answered. "I care only for you."

'His eyes met mine, searchingly, "Can it be true? Can you really feel this way?" he seemed to ask himself.

'"It is true," I answered him. "I want nothing more at this moment than to lie with you all night."

'"You do not know what you say," he insisted, "You are innocent, so unknowing. I would not give your parents anything to use against us."

'"Ryan," I protested, "it does not matter what my parents think. I love you. I know you love me too. Surely that is all that matters? You do love me - do you not?"

'He did not answer the question. Instead his expression closed and I heard the terrible sound of a mental barrier dropping between us.

'"Please," he said, refusing to look at me, "please - leave me alone - return to the safety of your bedchamber - I do not desire you."

'I was devastated. He had said that he longed to love me and yet now he was sending me away. I

172

had offered him all I had and he had not accepted it. He wanted me to leave him. I felt crushed. I got up and fled back to the house. Maybe I was ignorant of men, but the way I had felt, I was more than ready to be educated, and there was no-one else I would have teach me.'

Chapter Seventeen

From this time, Ryan kept his distance. If he had intended to hurt me, he could not have cut my heart deeper. He had said he wanted me, had he not? Then why was he acting this way? I knew from talk among the workers that Ryan was not inexperienced as I was. I had no knowledge of men at all. Perhaps that was it. Perhaps I was merely a child to him; of no interest to him. Maybe even his passionate kissing had been a fraud meant to frighten this foolish child away. But I had felt that passion; surely I could not have felt it so strongly if he had not?

'As the months passed by, Ryan and I were never alone, he made certain of it. I was so unhappy. I would have gone to him in the barn at night again but I did not have the courage. My heart could not take another rejection. If only I knew whether his behaviour that night had been the act - or his behaviour now. I thought I knew the answer but I dared not risk it. I resolved to devise a plan to discover the truth of the matter. I puzzled over this problem for quite a while. But I swear before God, I did believe in my heart that he must love me, and I prayed that I was right.

'Finally, as winter waned, I devised a plan. It was deceitful, I know, but I had to know one way or the other before I could think of the next step. I could not fail again.

'I waited impatiently until fate should present me with the right set of circumstances. The days passed so slowly until at long last the scene was set. I had been waiting for a day when Ryan was working in the fields alone, and out of sight of the house. Finally that day came. I saddled a horse, telling the household that I intended to ride into Hambledon but then I went in the opposite direction. This direction took me right past Ryan where he was working. I passed him not one hundred paces away but he gave no sign that he had seen me. He did not look up from his labours. I began to doubt my heart.

'Nevertheless I continued with my plan. No harm could come of it and I knew not what else to do. I rode the mare out of Ryan's sight, looking back to see if I could catch him watching me secretly, but no, he kept his gaze firmly on the ground that he was tending. Once I was well out of sight I dismounted from the mare, turned her back towards home and, picking up a branch from the track, I screamed out and shook it at her until she fled back the way we had come.

'Swiftly I arranged the scene. I lay on the ground, face down, arms outstretched, and waited. I did not dare look up to see if my ruse was working. I could not risk Ryan realising I was unharmed before he could show me his true feelings. It was a cruel trick, and I did feel ashamed, but I could not go on not knowing. I did not hear him coming on the soft track until he was almost upon me. I think my anxiety must have whitened my face for Ryan seemed to think me dead.

'As he drew near enough for me to hear his pounding feet, I heard him cry out, "Oh Mother of God, no! Please no! Madeleine!"

'He crashed to the ground beside me. I expected him to pick me up, but instead, he became very gentle. He made no attempt to move me, but carefully felt my limbs to see if my bones were smashed. After he had tenderly felt my skull, and began to stroke the side of my face, I could contain myself no longer. I opened my eyes.

'"Oh thank God, thank God," he breathed. Then he gathered me into his arms and sat there rocking me back and forth, his relieved breath sobbing in his throat. I had my answer. I did not like what I had done to him but, after all, it was no worse than the way he had been deceiving me. After a while he helped me to my feet, I trying to act dazed, although I was indeed so happy that I could have turned cartwheels. As we began to walk back Ryan tried desperately to re-adopt his false attitude but I was not fooled. I would show him that very night that he was the one being foolish.

'After dark, I crept once more to the barn doors. This time I would not accept his protests. And this time there was no pretence at sleep. Ryan was awake and sitting up the instant I entered the barn. I stood quietly for a moment looking down at him, and he could clearly see from my eyes that this time I was not to be fooled. He was waiting for me to speak first, but I could see from his discomfiture that he would soon have to break the silence that hung in the air, so I waited.

'"Madeleine," he began at last, "you truly make this so difficult for me - you cannot be found here.

What is it that you want of me?"

'I dropped to my knees beside him in the straw. "I want to be beside you - tonight and every night."

'"Oh God help me," he whispered. "What am I to do?" He wrenched his eyes away from my face, seemingly in turmoil. He would not, or could not, look at me. Then after a few silent moments, while I waited anxiously, he drew a deep shuddering breath and, still without looking at me, he reached out to me with one hand. I took it in mine and he tugged me, so that I fell into his arms.

'He held me close but he still had his eyes shut tight, and seemed to be fighting some inner battle, his breathing now heavy and strained. Then with a long sigh of surrender, he opened his eyes, and the love there was so plain to see that it made my heart soar with happiness. Then at last he kissed me. Once more I began to drown and once more I did not care. It was wonderful. Though I would have welcomed it, Ryan made no move to become more intimate, and I did not know how to. But he continued to kiss me, his arms wrapping me tightly against him, and for now that was enough. My body had flooded with a tide of passion at his touch and I could not control it. I would have lain there all night, answering his every need had he let me. But it would have been foolish, even I could see that. I may have gotten with child, I knew that much, and that would have been the end of Ryan.

'After a while he ceased to kiss me and when I looked up I could see torment in his eyes.

'"You must go now, leave me," he breathed, making no attempt to release me. "I cannot do this anymore." The words seemed wrenched from his mouth, "Please Madeleine - please go, while I can still let you."

'I could see that he meant it. I had my answer, the one I had wanted, and I could also see that my being here this way, with him naked beneath the rug and nothing else between us but my cotton night-gown was impossible for him. I knew little of the arts of the bedchamber but I knew that he was struggling to maintain my honour, so perhaps it was better that I left while I still could. It was a good, but in a way a sad thing, that Ryan possessed more willpower than I.

'I kissed him lightly one last time but he did not allow himself to respond. When I looked back at him from the doorway he had lain himself back down in the straw, his arm covering his eyes, his fist clenched.

'What I did not know at that moment was that I was observed leaving the barn. Eventually I guessed by the atmosphere and the unspoken accusations that filled the air the next day.

'It was the following night that I overheard my parents discussing the biggest mistake they were to make with Ryan. They were deciding to offer him a large sum of money if he would leave. How could they dismiss my feelings so? I knew this attempt would incense Ryan and I was right. This was when he finally lost all respect for them.

❧

Father went to the barn the next night to make his demands of Ryan. I had been unable to warn him of my father's intentions, and so I had hidden myself deep in the shadows of the hallway until my father appeared, then I followed him across the yard. I watched the encounter from just outside the barn

178

doors. Ryan was already to bed, and he sat up in surprise when Father walked in. I think it was a deliberate ploy on my parents' part for Father to call on him at this time, to have him at a disadvantage thereby, he being clad only in a rug. Ryan got to his feet as Father approached him, wrapping the rug about himself.

'Father and he regarded each other silently for a moment, and then Ryan spoke. "You have something to say?" he asked. In answer Father threw the pouch of money to the straw at Ryan's bare feet.

'I stared in interest. I had never seen Ryan's bare feet before. My feet compared to his, which were broad and strong looking, were pitifully narrow and skinny. I digress. I am, I confess, easily distracted by anything and everything to do with Ryan. That night, however, I was almost distracted by more than I had bargained for. Refusing to be intimidated by his situation, Ryan calmly dropped the rug which had been maintaining his dignity to the floor, with no show of embarrassment (indeed it was my father who looked away in embarrassment), and stooped unhurriedly to pull on his breeches. Fortunately for my innocence, but sadly for my inquisitive eyes, Father at that very moment had stepped into my line of vision, thus blocking Ryan from my sight.

'"What is this for?" Ryan asked, pointing at the pouch but making no attempt to pick it up.

'"It is for you to make a new start," Father answered.

'"Very generous."

'"There is however, a condition."

'"I thought there may be."

"This new start must be far from this place," Father announced.

'"And far from Madeleine?" Ryan asked.

'"That also."

'"No." Ryan's voice when he said this one word was quiet but so determined that my heart felt a surge of joy.

'"I do not make the situation clear," Father continued, "you are not being given a choice. You can either leave here in peace with this wealth, which to you will be more money than you will ever see again, or—"

'"Or what?" Ryan's voice had grown very cold now.

'"You will either leave this house and my daughter immediately; or steps will be taken to ensure that you leave here in a very sorry state, and as penniless as you came. But either way you will choose to leave, this I promise you."

"You are mistaken. I do not and will never choose to leave here unless Madeleine leaves with me. Her choice can only be her own."

'"She is but a child. You toy with her."

'"No, you give her no credit. She is not to be toyed with, she is full grown. And she is—" he paused, and then smiled a smile which must have infuriated Father, "She is mine."

'"Yours! I will see you dead before she is yours! Or do you tell me that you have already ruined her?"

'"I have not bedded her if that is what you ask," Ryan responded disdainfully.

'Father seemed to sigh with relief. "Then it is not too late. Now, will you leave in good health? Or must we take action to see that you leave?"

'"I will not leave without her, no."

'Father was not in any physical condition to threaten Ryan effectively and he knew this, so he merely pointed a finger and said, "I have told Margaret that you would not be easily bought. But, believe me, you will come to regret bitterly your defiance of us in this matter."

'"I may come to pay for this defiance, if your threats are real - but regret it? - no. Do your worst but I will still be here. I love your daughter as she loves me and I will never leave her. It is a pity you do not love her as much as I do." He picked up the pouch and thrust it back into Father's hands. "This—" he said, "merely shows how much she is worth to you - not how much you love her."

'Father looked thunderstruck but there was nothing more he could say, so he turned and left the barn. I had to sink back hurriedly into the shadows as he strode past me.

'I was so proud of Ryan defying my parents for the sake of our love. But I felt they would not give in so easily, and I feared what the threat Father had made might mean. I could not bear for any harm to come to Ryan. But surely they could see that I loved him and that, by harming him, they would just as surely harm me. I went into the barn.

'Ryan did not see me at first, he was so very angry. With his back to me he hit a wooden beam so hard, that I feared he would break his hand on it.

'"I did not want it to be this way!" he cried out. Then he saw me there and turned to me, "I did not want to tear you from your family," he said regretfully. He stopped and looked at me with indecision for a few moments. Then he dropped to his knees at my feet, his decision made. He took one of my hands in his, and with his eyes holding mine with their light, he said, "Madeleine, I have nothing to offer you except myself. If you become mine, you will lose the love of your family. I will be asking you to give up so much. But I can only swear that I love you - I think I have loved you for all time; become my wife and I will sacrifice anything, even my life's blood, to make you happy."

'I fell to my knees in turn and answered him as soon as I was able to speak. "Oh Ryan, believe me, I need nothing more in this world than you forever beside me. To become your wife is all I'll ever want."

'It was in truth all I wanted but I also felt that, once we were wed, my parents would cease their battle against us; surely once I had been made truly Ryan's no-one else would want me. Therefore as my husband he would be safer than he was now, for in truth I feared for him at this moment.

'We sat up half the night planning our secret wedding. As soon as arrangements could be made we would make our way to a disused abbey church that Ryan knew of. It was a long ride away but Ryan said that it was so beautiful he knew I would love it. Furthermore it would provide us with a suitable setting for the solemnity of our vows. I wished we could have left that night but I could see that it was not possible. However I was content that by the time my parents found out the deed would be done. After that nothing else would matter. [I wish she had been right.]

'After this night Ryan's behaviour changed towards me once more. He was openly affectionate to me and now he also seemed to feel the need to touch me often. He did not attempt to lie with me, though I often wished he would, but I no longer tried to tempt him to it. He wanted me to remain blameless even though my parents might not believe me to be so.'

These displays of affection from Ryan, may have been the cause of what happened next.

Chapter Eighteen

Had they limited their attempts to be rid of Ryan to bribery, I might have felt guilty about deceiving my parents and marrying behind their backs. But a few days later they played their most evil hand, knowing that time was running out for them. And this was the end of any sympathy I might have felt towards them. They denied all knowledge of what happened, of course, and we had little proof that the guilt lay at their door, but it was all too obvious to me that it was their doing. And, far from pulling Ryan and I apart, it united us more firmly than ever.

'Ryan had gone down to the village on an errand. Normally I would have accompanied him by choice but Mother said she had some chores for me that could not wait. Like a dutiful daughter I began to obey her, but when she left me to my own supervision I began to realise that these chores were in no way as urgent a matter as she had claimed. I suddenly had a knife of fear drive right through me and I knew for a certainty that, at that very moment, Ryan was walking into some terrible danger. I fled the house as if on wings, ran through the woods and down the meadow, finally crashing breathless through the hedge and into the lane behind the village.

A nightmare scene greeted me there. Ryan stood in the middle of the lane, like a stag at bay, surrounded by six blackguards who were obviously out to do him harm. I had not believed that my father would stoop to such a low and vile act. But it was plain that these ruffians were meant to persuade Ryan to change his mind and leave without me. I was more furious than I could remember ever having been before. And, like a mother lion whose cubs are threatened, I took a determined step forward. Ryan had seen me from the corner of his eye but he could not take his attention from the circling pack.

'"Madeleine!" he called out to me. "Stay back! There is nothing you can do here."

'Maybe he was right, maybe I could do nothing to help but neither could I just stand by and let this foul deed happen. By sending six men they had given Ryan no chance and my heart was frozen with fear as well as rage. I stood my ground. My appearance was obviously a surprise to the men as they were glancing my way in puzzlement. My mother had plainly been meant to distract me for longer.

'One of the men elected himself leader, and he spoke to me in a most condescending fashion. "Yes, Madeleine, my pretty thing, stay away—before we decide that we can have a more entertaining time with you than with the lad here." He licked his lips in a foul manner, quite turning my stomach.

'"Run Madeleine!" Ryan urged. "Back to the house!"

'I suppose in a way I made things even more difficult for him, in that he now feared for my safety as well as him own. But I could not leave him. Besides I was sure that these rogues were in the pay of my parents and, though I hated them both for that, I was also sure that these men had instructions that I was not to be harmed.

'I reached down and picked up a branch that lay on the grass next to the hedge and, with a scream that was frightening even to myself, such was its ferocity, I charged at the nearest man. I am pleased to say that I struck him a mighty blow to his skull, and he fell to the ground, all of a heap. Ryan took his chance and punched one man squarely on the nose so that this man also fell to the ground. Now there were only four, but the element of surprise had gone. Two of them turned on me, and the other two tried to push Ryan to the ground. I struggled, I bit and kicked and scratched, but to no avail; soon I was held fast by these two cowards. Ryan however was faring better than me. One of his assailants was bleeding from the mouth and the other was down on one knee. I began to hope.

'But the self-elected leader, one of those who held me, yelled, "Stop! If you care for this wench - stop at once!"

'Ryan stopped, his fist poised like a hammer in mid-air above his assailant. We all stood like a tableau of statues for a moment.

'"That is better," the leader said, and as he did so I could see the felled men rising to their feet, "Now you—" he pointed a grimy finger in Ryan's direction, "—will take your just punishment, like a man, with no resistance, or"—he pointed back at me—"will this fine lady will be accompanying us back to our lodgings to repay us for our trouble?"

'"No, Ryan!" I cried desperately, "They will not dare! Do not listen to him!"

'But Ryan would not risk it. Meeting my eyes across the lane he shook his head, then dropped his arms to his sides in mute surrender. The two men he had felled reached for him eagerly. They each took hold of one of his arms and twisted them cruelly behind his back. I was held fast and I could do nothing. My heart bled. Another of the villains advanced on Ryan menacingly. Ryan drew himself up, bracing himself for what was to come, his face set in grim lines. To my useless horror, the man began to beat him mercilessly with his fists.

'"No!" I cried out. "Leave him alone!" I pleaded with the men who held me, twisting in their grip, "I beg you! Please do not do this!"

'The leader leaned close to my ear, "Do not worry, my lovely, we will not kill him - not quite."

'I do not know for how long this terrible brutality was inflicted while I screamed in outrage but after a while Ryan was sagging in his captors' grasp, and he appeared senseless. They seemed to take this as a signal for now they let go of him, and he dropped heavily to the ground between them, and lay sprawled on his side, unmoving. I struggled with the men to escape and go to him but I could not break free. Still it would not stop though I begged and cried for God to make it do so. One of the men kicked Ryan in the back, bringing him unwillingly back to his senses. Then the man reached down and grasped Ryan's hair, pulling his head a few inches from the ground.

'He leaned close, and said the words that confirmed to me my parents' guilt. "Last chance, lad; do you swear to leave this place, and never return?"

'Ryan's eyes opened and the hurt there crushed my heart. But he said, loud enough for me to hear, "No - I will not."

'Immediately it began again, all three men using their boots, fetching Ryan hefty kicks, shouting encouragement to each other while he lay helpless. It was such a cowardly act that my blood felt like fire. The blows continued to fall until his spirit was roused, and he tried to get up. But every time he got to his hands and knees, in response to their shouts and taunts, another kick would send him sprawling once more.

'A cold hand of fear clutched at my heart. I could see that the blackguards had lost control of themselves. Ryan was being beaten to death before my very eyes! I knew he could not survive much more of this treatment.

'"Stop!" I shouted, "You said you would not kill him!"

'With some difficulty the leader tore his greedy eyes away from their feast of violence. He seemed to have to snatch himself from some other world.

'"Yes - I did say this." He yelled to the other men, "Enough! Before he is killed! We were not to kill him." The men, reluctantly, one by one, ceased kicking him, and I drew a deep breath of relief for I could see that he still moved - he was not dead. The leader spoke again to the pack of three who still circled Ryan threateningly while he was once more dragging himself to his hands and knees. "We were however to prevent him from taking the delights of a woman!" One of the attackers grinned at us, and, to my awful dismay and jeers from the other two, he drove a brutal kick between Ryan's legs from behind. This drew a cry from Ryan that tore at my heart, like an axe cleaving a tree trunk. He fell to the ground again, bringing his legs up and curling himself into a ball. Then the assailant leaned down, and shouted into Ryan's face, "Now you will choose to leave!"

188

'I had been right about one thing. As soon as they had finished with Ryan, they pushed me aside and fled. I was not to be harmed. I ran to Ryan where he lay. It broke my heart to see him try to get up, for he could not do it. I tried to help him but it hurt him so. I longed to soothe him with my hands, but he could not endure to be touched. His breathing was coming in ragged gasps, and he pleaded with me, "No—no—Madeleine—let me lie—let me lie. Please—leave me."

'In the end, though I could hardly bear to, I left him where he was and went to fetch some help. I found two of Father's workers in the buildings, and, chivvying them for their slowness, I took them back to where Ryan lay. He was as I had left him and I thanked God that the varlets had not returned.

'The two workmen lifted Ryan, though he still protested at the touch of their less than gentle hands. I knew that the journey was hurting him further but I had to get him to safety. So they half-carried, half-dragged him, up the hill and back through the woods, and at my instructions finally laid him on the straw in the barn, where he once more gratefully curled up on his side, legs drawn up, moaning softly.

'I could only think of one person to help him - Nancy - so I ran and fetched her. Her first reaction, on seeing him, was horror but she managed to persuade him to lie on his back so that she could assess the damage to his body. After we had removed his shirt, I could see that his abdomen was already blackened with bruising. But before Nancy could do anything for him, a terrible spasm took him so that he rolled onto his side once more, gasping in the throes of pain. At this Nancy was forced to send me from the barn, so that she could attend to him. I had truly been no help at all, his distress causing me to cry out in sympathy.

'She did not allow me to re-enter until she had tended all his injuries, and he was decently covered with his rug, looking a little less drawn. But as she let me back in, she confided quietly to me, news that turned my very soul to ice.

'She said, "The blackness of his skin points to bleeding deep within his body. I can do no more for him, and the morning will tell - if he will live."

'My heart stuttered and I almost swooned at these words, waves of dread stopping my breath, but I tried not to let Ryan see. I resolved that for once, I would be strong for his sake.

'I lay with Ryan all through the night, holding him when he could let me, and crying fresh tears whenever a new jolt of pain shook him. It seemed that the night went on forever.

'But finally the sun began to rise and he seemed to pass into a normal sleep so that Nancy pronounced that he would indeed survive, and relief swept through my being.

'My parents did not know how close they came that night to fearful harm at my hands. And at ten o' clock my mother appeared at the barn door. I was on my feet in an instant, ready to defend Ryan with my life.

'"What do you want here?" I almost screamed at her.

'"Madeleine, you have been out here all night. We are afeared for your reputation."

'"Fear not for my reputation;" I replied, "fear more for your own safety."

'"My dear child," she tried to soothe me, "you are distraught. What has happened?"

'Even as she spoke, she was trying to step around me so that she would be able to see Ryan and I knew then that she had come to gloat over the results of her vindictiveness. I stepped towards her threateningly, and my eyes looked straight into her soul. God help me, at that instant I truly knew the meaning of hatred. My hands ached with a need for vengeance. She too saw inside my mind, and something she saw writ there caused her to drop her gaze and hurriedly depart.

'Ryan had, of course, been disturbed from his much-needed sleep by all this, and he lay with his eyes open, not yet strong enough to sit up. But at least he now looked truly alive.

'"My lady," Nancy began, "It becomes apparent to me—"

'"No Nancy," Ryan interrupted her, his voice still sounding pained.

'"Do the pair of you think I have no thoughts of my own in my head?" I cried. "Do you think I do not know who is responsible for this cowardly act? All I ask you, Ryan, is will you wish to leave me now, for I could not blame you if you did?"

'"I will be here for as long as you want me," he answered.

'"Then please excuse me; I have an errand to attend to." I looked back at him to see if he had any further objections to voice. He said nothing, but the suffering burning in his eyes inflamed me. "Very well," I said, and I left the barn.

'I confronted my parents in the drawing room. I gave them no chance to speak.

'"I will not waste my breath accusing you of this crime, for I know you will deny all blame. However, I will tell you this. I know what you have done. Should any further harm come to Ryan then you had best do the same to me, for I will surely kill they who harm him. This I swear by God. Do you not yet

191

understand, Father, what you do to him you also do to me. And, if you thought to bully him into leaving me where your bribery failed, then you have failed once more. I also tell you this: I love Ryan more than life itself and, had you succeeded in driving him away, then my life would have no meaning and I would end it."

'With this I turned and left the sight of their startled faces. I returned to the barn, and saw Ryan lying there once more in a peaceful sleep. I sat beside him and pressed one of his hands between both of mine, kissing it tenderly. And at that moment I knew the truth of what I had said to my parents. I loved him more than life itself. Had he died or left without me, then life would have held no meaning and I would have ended it.'

Ryan recovered sufficiently from his injuries, so that two weeks later he and Madeleine were married at Milton Abbey church.

You may ask whether or not Edwin was ever persuaded by Margaret to try the same kind of bullying tactics on Madeleine. I will tell you. It was very common in those days, and quite accepted, for parents to thrash their unruly offspring, even the girls. It was usually done with a stiff cane which bruised but did not cut. They tried this only once on Madeleine to try and force her to renounce her love for Ryan. As a result Ryan terrified Margaret so much that she never dared to try it again.

June 1638 (two months after the wedding. By now they obviously realised that Madeleine was not, after all, going to tire of him of her own accord.)

'I was called to the drawing room unexpectedly this evening. Ryan was still out in the fields at this late hour, because of the urgent need to gather in the hay harvest. Mother and Father were both present in the room, she looking somewhat smug; Father, on the other hand, seemed rather shame-faced and would not look at me. There were also two of Father's casual labourers in the room. They were of the rougher type of men who worked on the farm only during harvesting. I was very puzzled as to what this all meant.

'Then Mother spoke to me in a very sanctimonious manner. "Madeleine, I have been discussing with your father the fact that you have become totally wayward and out of hand. You show us no respect. You have had no discipline in years, and this is why we find ourselves in this predicament. You need to be brought to heel. We have been very patient with you, allowing you more than enough time to learn from your mistakes, but now you must be taught obedience once and for all. Your marriage to this Irish peasant will be annulled immediately. Do you understand?"

'I sighed, not this again. "No," I said wearily, "I do not understand. When will you both understand? Our vows were made and meant for life. No-one will part us."

'"You will learn differently," she continued. "When I was a child any disobedience was curbed as yours will be curbed now. You have been getting away with your hard-headedness for quite long enough."

'I was stunned and horrified for she signalled to the two men and, as they came at me, she produced a long thick cane from behind her back and I realised what she meant to do. She meant to beat me! I tried to escape through the door, but the two men barred my way.

'I ran to my father in desperation and grasped his hands, pleading: "Father you cannot allow this thing!—Please!—Father!" But he would not look at me.

'"It is no use, child," she said. "Your father has been advised by me in this matter." At this the two men took hold of my arms, and propelled me across the room to the big oak table. They pushed me face down against the polished surface. I was very afraid at this moment, and I could see my rapid breaths forming a pool of mist on the shiny wood. She smacked the cane against her skirts as she approached me.

'Ryan told me later that he had been working in the hay meadows, two fields away from the house, when he had seen the stout figure of Nancy rushing towards him as fast as she was able. He ran to meet her. Gossip in the servants' quarters had alerted her to my mother's wicked scheme. He said she was puffing so heavily that he feared for her health but, between gasps, she managed to tell him enough so that he made off for the house at a dead run.

'The first I knew of this was when the door to the dining room suddenly crashed open with such force that it banged into the wall. At that moment she was standing over me, the cane raised in her clenched fist, ready to strike the first blow. That blow never landed on its intended target for she immediately turned it on Ryan. But his charge was such that he was upon her before she could do anything. She let out a startled shriek as he snatched the cane from her hand and snapped it in two. She ran to Father who looked terrified. Wasting no time, Ryan advanced on the two men who held me. The ferocity of his expression was such that the men, who had been told that they must merely restrain a young woman, had no stomach for a fight so they let go of me. Raising their hands to Ryan in a placating gesture they dodged around him and made off through the door. They must have kept running for I never saw either of them again. Ryan took me in his arms and held me close. I looked up at his face, clinging just as tightly.

'"Are you all right?" he asked, anxiously.

'"Yes," I replied. "She did not touch me."

'"As well she did not!" Ryan turned to face her, so angry that his words spat at her like snake venom: "This time it is best you heed my warning! Do not ever dare come near her again! For if you ever lay a hand on her again I will kill you! You may escape justice for your treatment of others—" He let go of me and stepped up close to her. She drew back involuntarily at the naked rage in his eyes as he continued, "—but if you ever touch Madeleine again, do not doubt me - you will die!"

'"Edwin!" she screamed. "Do something in my defence!" But Father was too afraid for his frail bones, and he did not move.

'"He at least perhaps feels some of the shame that you should feel," Ryan continued, his blazing eyes inches from hers. He raised a clenched fist above her, and I could see that she feared he would hit her. He held it close to her face so that she blanched. "This time," he said, "I have saved you from yourself but understand - these bare hands will destroy you if you ignore this warning a second time."

'Even when we had reached our bedchamber, Ryan was still distraught. He paced the room, unable to calm himself. I began to undress in the hope of distracting him. This ruse worked, and soon he cradled me in his arms, stroking the bare skin of my back.

'"She should thank God that she did not mark you," he said, his eyes dark.

'That night, his love-making was so tender and so reverent that it brought tears to my eyes. Never was a woman so loved by any man.'

Another memory has been pushing its way into my consciousness over the last few days. It was not a day of great import, with regard to any dramatic happenings, but it was very special for another reason. I had bought a new quartz crystal and it seemed to have the power to bring memories out in fine detail. Here is the memory in its entirety.

September 1638 (five months after the wedding)

'The bringing in of a successful harvest is always celebrated with a market and fair. This year Ryan and I were able to attend it for the first time as husband and wife. I was very excited, and I harried Ryan mercilessly through his chores so that we could set off. We took a picnic basket and with almost all the villagers we sat on the banks of the stream, in the long grass, to consume our food and drink.'

This was the point at which my new crystal performed its magic. I shared this wonderful experience so closely with Madeleine, and the scene seemed so real to me that I could almost believe I had travelled back in time. Ryan was beside me and I was truly able to study his face up close for what seemed like a long time, as though I was seeing him through my own eyes rather than using Madeleine's thoughts to relay information to me. As Ryan sat beside me I could see the side view of his face as he gazed at the water. He was sitting in characteristic pose, legs bent in front of him, one arm resting across his knees, that hand draped casually over them, the other arm bracing him against the grass. My eyes travelled back to his face, so clear to me in every detail. His big eyes with their beautiful blue irises and heavy lids; his aristocratically shaped brows; his nose, straight and finely chiselled; his generous mouth, the full lower lip lending to his face a permanent, slightly crestfallen look; and his even skin tone, with its dark beard shadow. All these features were breathtaking in their clarity. I could see the texture of his hair, its colour that of a raven, almost blue/black. His neck showed defined muscles which then blended into wide shoulders, giving an overwhelming impression of strength. Still I was given more time to look. His throat was exposed, because the tie of his shirt was undone, and I could glimpse threads of fine hair at the top of his chest.

I dared not move for some while, for fear of dissolving the vision. I felt completely inside

Madeleine, but I did not know if I could control it - I tried. I reached out a hand, which looked and felt like my own, and I could touch his arm, clad in the heavy cotton of his shirt sleeve. I could actually feel the rough folds of the full sleeves beneath my fingertips. Then my hand touched his where it dangled from his knees. As I did I noticed that his breeches on this day were made of leather, soft and well-creased with wear. He turned and smiled at me. I smiled back. Then the image faded. I tried to recapture it, but it was gone.

❧❧❧

'We began to walk through the market. Underfoot, because of the shortage of rain, the street was inches deep in dust, coating our shoes. But above this the village looked so different, bedecked as it was with streamers, flags, and banners. And there was so much to see, so many wonderful things for sale. There were reams of woollen cloth, hung game birds with bright plumage, rabbits and hares, and even the occasional half-hog. There were rainbows of ribbons, pots and pans, cheeses, horse-bells and jugs of ale. Some of the stall-holders were village people selling their wares but others, such as the knife-grinder, made their living travelling around the countryside with all their trappings. I could not help but touch the ribbons for their colours were so varied and rich. [They would have seemed quite dull though to modern eyes.] After a while I realised that Ryan had grown silent beside me. Looking at him I could easily read his thoughts. He knew that this was the first year of my life when I had not been sought after by my parents to accompany them to the fair. And that on each previous visit I would have had bought for me anything I had desired. He was dwelling, I knew, on how much he perceived that I had given up to be with him. He was wishing, I am certain, that he could buy me what he thought I wanted. I laughed softly, as if at myself.

'"It is strange," I said, "how these things no longer hold such attraction for me. They seem childish now that I have you." Ryan smiled. I think he knew the statement to be contrived but he appreciated my intention. [I interrupt Madeleine at this point to recount to you a rather strange feeling I experienced as I re-lived this walk through the stalls. As we passed the knife-grinder, I saw his face as clearly as I had Ryan's. He was a small, weaselly man, dirty, and almost toothless. His face was creased and rough, and I felt an unaccountable uneasiness as he looked back at me. I had never felt this kind of fear before during a regression. And I actually felt myself physically turn my head, on the bed where I was meditating, as if to glance back at him. When we passed the ale stall, the same distasteful person was lounging there as if he had darted ahead to be there in front of us. Ryan did not seem to notice, but I felt a chill run through me. As myself, and as Madeleine, for now it was hard to distinguish between the two of us, I let go of Ryan's hand and slid my arm more securely though his, drawing us into a closer contact. I felt safer immediately but I could not help but glance back again, and sure enough the man's eyes were still fastened to me like leeches. I snuggled yet closer to Ryan's comforting presence, and now he too looked back to see the reason for my unease. As he saw the man he seemed to share some of my concern, for I felt his arm muscles tighten protectively under my hand. Nothing further happened then but I wonder if at some point I will be shown the reason for this nameless fear.]

'We strolled on towards the fair. Here competitions raged. Rivals strove to be stronger, faster and better than each other. There was bare-knuckled fist fighting which seemed to disgust Ryan. I found it distasteful myself and certainly did not try to persuade him to take part. The violence was senseless and brutal. This was reflected in the mood of the crowd who bayed for blood as they watched. On the far side of the meadow there was a horse race in progress, and we stood and watched this with great interest for a while. The animals taking part were many and varied. They ranged from tiny hairy ponies, ridden bareback by small wiry boys who clung to their backs like limpets, to giant dray horses with massive feet who pounded past the ponies as if they would trample them unnoticed. I knew that one of Ryan's dearest wishes was to own a horse. If I had but possessed one I would have given it to him gladly.

'There were various feats of strength taking place and I grasped Ryan's arm excitedly. "Surely," I pleaded, "you must take part in one of these?" He was surprisingly reluctant, not relishing the attention of the villagers. He resisted my attempts at persuading him to join in the single-handed tug o' war that took place over the stream so that the loser was pulled into the water. Finally, after much cajoling from me, determined as I was to show him off, he agreed to become a contestant in the wagon-pulling competition. This consisted of pulling wooden carts along which were gradually loaded with more and more barrels of water, making them heavier and heavier. The man who could move the heaviest of them, by pulling it along over a distance of ten paces would be the winner.

'I was amazed and - I admit - proud of Ryan's strength as again and again he threw his shoulder into the harness and the cart unwillingly followed him over the line. When the cart had been loaded to its capacity there was still one seemingly as strong as Ryan. It was decided to hold a head to head pull. Another cart was fetched. They would drag a cart each, side by side, and the winner would be he who towed his cart the furthest across the rough grass.

'Both men were given a short rest, so Ryan dropped to the grass beside me where I sat. He lay on his back, stretched out, his arms crossed over his face to shield his eyes from the bright sun. I could see that his shirt was damp in places with sweat and clung to him. The hair on his brow was wet with it and it was curled into glossy tendrils, while beads of moisture rolled down his face, falling onto the bone-dry ground where it was greedily sucked up by the thirsty grass. I took the water flask from the picnic basket, and offered it to him. He took but a few sips and then upended the remainder over his head.

'After a few minutes, the two men were called to their task. Ryan's rival was Thomas Hendry, a beefy man weighing more than Ryan. But I felt that some of his bulk was due, not to muscle, but to his liking for ale. Thomas was red in complexion and red in temper. As they were fastened into their harnesses he tried to taunt Ryan into rashness. This I knew, and could have told him, was a fruitless task. Ryan was never swayed by such behaviour. As the starter dropped his flag Ryan and Thomas leaned into their harnesses. Thomas threw his whole weight into his and his wagon jolted into forward movement, picking up a rolling speed close behind him, as every vein and sinew stood out over his face, neck and arms. Ryan however took up a much steadier pull, his wagon moving much more gradually and smoothly. Thomas heaved, throwing himself constantly against the straps, striving for greater and greater speed. Soon he was twenty paces ahead of Ryan, who in contrast, moved with a steady rhythm, his strong legs pacing relentlessly forward. People began cheering Thomas as he forged ahead, seeing an obvious winner. But to me the outcome was plain. Thomas pulled his wagon in jerks and starts to the fifty pace mark, and then, thinking he had done enough and exhausted anyway, he dropped to the ground between the shafts to the acclaim of his neighbours. They began to gather around him in congratulation.

'Then, quite suddenly, they realised that Ryan was still coming, and catching up fast now. They urged Thomas to his feet, especially those that had placed their wager on him, as Ryan's cart was now only twenty paces behind. Thomas staggered to his feet, reeling breathlessly and endeavoured to re-start the cart, but he could not do it with muscles that had now turned to water. He struggled futilely as Ryan overtook him and had no choice but to admit defeat as Ryan pulled his cart another twenty paces. Ryan had won! I rushed forward and threw my arms around him. He was breathing heavily and smelled muskily of sweat. I found the natural scent of him very appealing and I breathed it in greedily. Ryan's prize was a squealing, half-grown hoglet.

'We had perforce to make our way home now, for our prize was an unwilling captive and thrashed relentlessly in Ryan's arms. We struggled homewards, Ryan carrying his wriggling prize, both of us thinking of the banquet to come. However, I admit, though Ryan would not like to, I think, that in the midst of the woodland we took pity on our prize and set it free. It trotted off, grunting happily and was soon lost to sight.

'Ryan claimed an alternative prize from me, one I was happy to give, as I was still aroused by the sight of his strength and power and the scent of his labours. It was a truly wonderful day, and even the black looks evident from the dining room window as Mother watched us approach could not spoil it for us.'

Chapter Nineteen

I have decided to hold the 'farewell' ceremony. I'm not sure if I'm ready for it but I'm going ahead.

Later. It will take me a long time to recover from this latest emotional onslaught. I am a long way yet from being ready to say goodbye either to Madeleine or Ryan.

I bought two candles especially for the occasion - blue ones - as that was the favourite colour of both of them. I had waited until I had an evening alone for I felt it should be done after dark. I lit the candles and began to meditate. I found myself saying, 'Ryan and Madeleine, I want to commemorate your spirits in this way. I know both of you are now free, and have moved on, but by re-uniting you this way you can say goodbye to each other - through me.

Madeleine spoke through me; 'Ryan, I loved you with my whole heart and soul, this you must know. And I know you loved me the same way, for you came back for me, to give me an easy passage into the beyond. I have never forgiven myself for not listening to your warnings, and I regret so much causing you to go through such awful physical pain. Please, please forgive me what I cannot forgive myself. Do not forget me through a hundred lifetimes. I will always love you. Goodbye my love.'

I couldn't go on for some while. I didn't know how I would give Ryan a chance to speak. But, instead, I was given what I consider to be a very rare and precious privilege - I was given Ryan's thoughts and feelings to share. Ryan's perception of events was very interesting, and some of his experiences explain a lot about his character, so I will repeat them here from his point of view.

Ryan's father died in Ireland before Ryan was born; after that his mother worked herself into an early grave, trying to stop her children from starving. She managed this for twelve years but then she too died. Ryan was left with two sisters. One was older than him by two years and the other was his twin. At twelve years old, having already suffered a life of hardship and deprivation, Ryan became the man of the house and the sole breadwinner. There was so little work, even for a strong lad, and none at all for the girls. He worked all day, sometimes half the night, for the local wealthy land-owners in order to feed himself and his sisters.

This was when Ryan had his first real taste of the arrogance of most rich people of that time, his mother having protected him from it as well as she could. Ryan only came to realise after her death (as many of us do), just how much his mother had sacrificed for him and his sisters. She had even scraped together enough money for him to be taught to read and write, he had such a passion for it. But as a boy of only twelve years old, he could only do so much, provide so much, for his sisters. He was forced to call on those better off to beg for food for them. His sisters could not do this, for they would have been used in a much worse manner than Ryan was, and he was treated badly enough. For the most part they only amused themselves by humiliating him. They sometimes forced him to fight a bigger, stronger opponent from amongst those in their own employ, promising him a great prize if he should win, and sometimes he did win. Other times he went home with a bloody nose or worse. He soon learned to defend himself for he had to in order to survive. If he lost he went home empty handed, while if he won he was seen off with a few kitchen scraps. Sometimes the rich men's sons would entertain themselves at his expense, taunting him until he gratified them by responding with anger.

One such time, when Ryan called at a kitchen door to ask for food, the owner's three sons waylaid him on his way out. They were aged ten years, fourteen years, and nineteen years, and they surrounded him, barring his way, pushing him back and forth, shouting taunts in his face. Finally he lost his temper and he launched himself furiously at the eldest lad. He thought that somehow, if he could best the biggest of them, the others would back off and leave him be. But these upper class bullies had no intention of fighting fairly, and so the other two brothers threw themselves on Ryan's back. Ryan had become tough, and he was big for his age, but these three together were too much for him. He found himself helplessly pinned down by their combined weight. The eldest one, ruefully holding a bruised nose, got up, and all three dragged Ryan to his feet. The two younger ones held his arms, and he could probably have struggled out of their grasp, but the eldest clutched him by his hair, keeping his head well pulled back so that he had no chance to kick out at them.

They forced him onward this way, over to the deep farm pond, egging each other on, the eldest one saying, 'Little thug! We shall teach you some manners! Come on! We shall drown him, just like papa does to all the unwanted kittens and puppies!'

Ryan was terrified. He had not yet learned to swim, and in any case it did not appear that he would have that chance. The three boys waded out, dragging Ryan with them, the farm ducks quacking angrily and scattering at their approach. Soon the smallest boy was up to his chin in the dirty water. Then the eldest lad pulled at Ryan's hair and, with the two others still holding his arms, he was forced over backwards into the murky depths. He could not see anything through the mud particles that swirled up from the bottom. He tried to hold his breath for as long as he could, his legs thrashing futilely as his body fought instinctively to bring him back into the air. Finally he had no more breath, and he involuntarily swallowed a mouthful of the rank water, its taste brackish and vile in his throat. Suddenly they pulled him up and he gasped desperately for air. But before he could really regain his breath, they ducked him under yet again. Strangely, he could still hear their voices, even while he was under the surface. They were muffled and muted, but he knew they were laughing. Ryan thought he was going to die, as he once more began helplessly to swallow mouthfuls of the water which flooded, cold and leaden, into his lungs. Once more they pulled him up, only to push him under once more. This time Ryan ceased struggling and went limp, for his oxygen-starved muscles were weak and no longer able to obey him. At last the lads realised they had gone too far. They were not really murderers.

He felt their hands let go of him, hearing dimly, as though through a fog, 'Come! That is enough! One of his sort will die soon enough in any event. I believe he has learned his lesson, and he will not trouble us again.'

Ryan burst through the grey surface of the pond like a blowing whale. By the time he had found his feet and half-stood, half-floated, long enough to cough the water out of his lungs and fill them instead with life-giving air, his three attackers had made off. He could see them disappearing into the farmhouse. Ryan fought his way to the bank, feeling horribly powerless, his stomach sickened by all the filthy water he had ingested. He collapsed onto the bank, retching, and lay there, cold and shivering in the mud until he regained sufficient strength to get to his feet and leave.

Even as he had lain there, he had been thinking that he must apparently learn to grow a tough skin, as well as a tough body, in order to survive in this cruel world. He must learn to ignore them all, and not let them hurt him with their words. No-one cared, no-one cared at all. He came to understand this sad truth at a very young age.

I interrupt Ryan's story here, because this incident has made clear to me something that had been puzzling me in another memory. This narrative is just like a jigsaw puzzle to me, pieces constantly dropping into place, making a whole picture. I will let Madeleine tell the story I refer to.

Sixteenth June 1638 (Ryan's seventeenth birthday)

'Up until this day, I had been unable to imagine seeing Ryan frightened. I am sure there were times when he was afraid but he never showed it in his actions, or his expression. I believe this was something he had trained into himself, a necessary device for self-preservation. For in the environment he had been born to any sign of weakness was very dangerous. Only the strong survived in his world. I think this ability to remain apparently calm in the face of danger or adversity, had saved him on many occasions.

'This day I had planned a surprise for him on his birthday. We rode the horses, at my direction, to a lake but five miles from the house. It was a place from my happier childhood, before Margaret had come, and it was very beautiful. Ryan had never seen it before and I was very excited at this rare chance to show him something new. All through the journey I felt laughter bubbling on my lips, and I must have seemed like a playful child to him.

'I had timed our arrival at the lake very carefully, for just this once I had some small piece of magic to reveal to him. We emerged through the trees at the right moment, just as the low morning sun slanted its glittering rays across the still surface of the water. And now here was the magic. Spread in front of us was a carpet of diamonds, shattering the air with shards of white flashing light. I heard Ryan gasp with amazement at this display of fiery splendour. We stopped for a while, taken by the wonder of it. Then, as we drew closer, the trick was revealed. Not diamonds after all, but a small pebble beach littered with quartz stones, each stone a mockery of its precious cousin, the diamond. For a few seconds each day, when the sun was low in the east, these lowly crystals became aristocrats. We dismounted from the horses and Ryan delightedly gathered a pocketful of these fallen stars. He said he would polish them and make them into a necklace for me. We stood for a few moments breathing deeply of the clean, moisture-filled air. Then Ryan took me in his arms, and thanked me for this surprise.

'I told him that the surprise was not over yet, and that I had a small boat hidden in the reeds. I told him of the tiny island out in the centre of the lake - and that it was to be our own world for the day, cut off from all others. As I spoke, I began to unpack the wicker baskets we had carried behind our saddles, and so absorbed was I with removing food, drink, and a blanket that I did not notice any apprehension Ryan may have felt. By the time my attention was returned to him, he appeared as stoic as ever.

'We pulled the rowing boat free of the reeds, loaded it with our provisions and climbed into it. Ryan's hands were steady as he took up the oars and began to row. I had no inkling that he was concerned, for every part of him was tightly controlled. I was a strong swimmer, having come to this place with my mother [her real mother, Rebecca], since I was a small child and, like most who are at home in deep water, it did not occur to me that others might not share this confidence. So, as we reached the mid point between the shore and the island and the deepest part of the lake, I became mischievous. I had a vision in my head of Ryan and I playing in the water together, of slick naked bodies entwining in the cool water. So I suddenly stood up, uncaring of the precariousness of this action, and I began to unlace my gown.

'The boat began to rock to my movements and as I started to pull the gown off over my head my pleasant reverie was pierced by Ryan's voice, sounding unnaturally harsh, "Madeleine, stop! You will fall!"

'I laughed, my voice muffled by the gown, for falling into the water and being 'rescued' by Ryan, was my intention. But, as my dress landed in the bottom of the boat and Ryan was revealed to me once more, I could hear his gasps and, looking at him, I could see that he was genuinely alarmed - no it was more than that - he was truly afraid. As the boat rocked more violently, threatening to capsize, his hands dropped the oars and grasped the sides of the boat, his knuckles white with the force of his grip. I was stunned, then mortified. He looked so vulnerable to me.

'Swiftly I dropped down to a safer position, placing my hands on his knees, saying, "Ryan, I am sorry. It is all right, I am safe. Even had I fallen, I am a strong swimmer."

'He had been staring fixedly into the bottom of the boat but now he looked back up at me, unblinking. His rigid expression did not alter. As the boat steadied, with deliberation he pulled his hands one at a time from the side of the boat, then picked up the oars once more. Silently he began to row but he turned the boat and headed it back to the shore. I was puzzled and concerned. Although he remained speechless until we were on dry land again he was obviously not angry with me, for he hugged me tightly and did not seem to want to let me go. Rather, he seemed angry with himself. He never gave me an explanation and I did not press him, for he seemed desperately to want no reminder of the incident. I was, I hope, sensitive to his needs, as he had been to mine on so many occasions, and we had our picnic on the sparkling beach, returning home hours later, replenished as always by our time together.'

⚜

Obviously Ryan, because of the cruel treatment shown to him by the three boys, had become afraid of deep water. Sitting in the small boat with Madeleine as it rocked wildly, I'm sure he could already taste the sour water as it forced its way down his throat to fill his lungs and stomach; and once again feel his muscles become powerless, as life drained from them; feel the pain in his chest from holding his breath for too long. His pulse would have been racing and he would have had to fight to prevent himself from crying out in fear. No-one could blame him for these feelings. He was, as I knew, quite happy in shallow streams, but deep water was dark and dangerous to him.

This picture I have in my mind of him looking so vulnerable as he stared up at Madeleine in the boat, is very emotive to me and, even now, I want to put my arms around him, especially as I, unlike Madeleine at the time, know the justifiable reason for this fear. It was typical of him, though, that he did not allow this fear to freeze his blood. He overcame it, controlled it, enough anyway to take them both out of the danger he perceived under the calm surface of the lake.

Back to Ryan's story

He continued to try his best to feed his family, the time coalescing into a haze of dispirited tiredness, the days and nights merging, and also experiencing a growing, if unjustified sense of guilt, frustration, and failure. (Even today, as a mega-star, this man, as a result of his misplaced sense of not doing enough in his life as Ryan, pushes himself to the limits and beyond, never feeling he has achieved enough. The danger of this, is of course - burn-out. And this is one of the reasons why I know I have to meet him again in a situation where I will be able to tell him all about his past life.)

His elder sister sickened and died a year later from smallpox, and his twin sister grew steadily weaker from malnutrition. It broke his heart to see her sinking lower and lower, all the time feeling powerless to help her, while feeling guilty because he could not. The situation was made worse by the 'no win' circumstances. If he gave all his food to his sister it would not be many days before he would no longer have the strength to work, and then they would have had no food at all. And quite often he was paid in food, to be eaten in the middle of the day when he could not give it to his sister. Therefore he felt as if he had more than his fair share. He came home one evening, just before their fourteenth birthday, to find his twin dying. He held her in his arms for over an hour until she died, and then, only pausing long enough to bury her, he walked to the docks and left Ireland on a cargo ship bound for Southampton. He was determined to try and make a new life for himself.

(This knowledge has explained something else to me. It has made me understand why Ryan did not put more pressure on Madeleine to leave her home and go with him. For if he had threatened to go without her, she would have succumbed to the threat. It was because he had too much experience already of starvation and hardship. He doubted his own ability to provide for Madeleine, and could not stand the thought that he might have to watch helplessly as she died too. At least while she remained under her father's roof this would not happen.)

His very first encounter with Englishmen after landing was not destined to endear them to him. He was wearily plodding down a narrow country lane, having covered twenty miles from the port, not knowing where he might find food or shelter, and with a growing terrified feeling of being totally alone in the world, with no-one to care whether he lived or died. He missed the camaraderie of life on board ship even though the work had been so hard. But he knew he was not cut out to be a sailor for he lived in constant fear of falling overboard.

Suddenly, from behind the tall hedge that flanked the lane, he heard a frightful commotion. There was the excited baying of hounds and the petrified sound of an animal in mortal fear. There was a small gap at the bottom of the hedge, and Ryan scrambled through it. His actions from then on were purely instinctual, with no reasoning, for here at last was a creature more powerless than himself. In the corner of the meadow, where the tall hedge of the perimeter of the field made a triangle with the five bar gate entrance into another field, there was a trapped and sweat-soaked deer and her new-born fawn. The fawn was all wide, terrified eyes and long, unsteady legs. The doe would normally have jumped the gate with ease but her fawn could not, so she stayed with it. She faced a small pack of hunting hounds as she tried futilely to protect her infant. This pathetic yet heroic display of maternal courage touched Ryan's heart deeply and he felt not fear of the pack but fury.

The doe was already bleeding from several bites from the dogs and she was bleating pitifully.

Ryan tore a thick branch from the hedgerow and, putting his back to the flagging deer, he began to swing this weapon at the circling pack. They backed off, confused by this attack from a human.

Ryan took advantage of this, and yelled at them, 'Get back! Get back!' They retreated further, and he used this respite to dive at the gate, dragging and lifting it through the long grass as it protested on its rusty hinges until the gap was enough, and the deer, sensing escape, bounded through and sped across the next field, closely followed by her fawn. The hounds surged forward but Ryan continued to hold them off, swinging the branch like a sword.

Then came the sound of horsemen. There were ten of them and they pounded across the field, their shouts reaching him. They could see their quarry escaping and this wild figure slashing at their hounds with a branch. They were very angry at this disruption to their day's sport, and they drove their horses into the mêlée, scattering the hounds. Ryan was buffeted by them until, with a furious shout, one rider brought his fist down heavily on Ryan's shoulder, knocking him to the ground. Hooves flashed at him, one catching him a sharp blow to his leg, and Ryan would bear the imprint of its shoe on his thigh for many weeks. But as he lay bruised and battered in the grass, he turned and had the great satisfaction of seeing the deer and her fawn reach the far side of the field, and disappear into the woodland there, well ahead of her pursuers. Ryan picked himself up, and very sensibly for his own preservation, scrambled back through the hedge, and set off down the lane at his best speed. Although his leg pained him he felt his spirits lift and there was a bounce in his step, even though he glanced back over his shoulder many times to make sure that he had not now become the prey of the hunt, having deprived them of their original victim. He supposed that the plight of the poor deer and her baby had made him feel a little less helpless. There were after all others worse off than he.

After a worrying interval during which time he had to sleep outdoors and gather what food he could from the hedgerows and fields, he found work on a farm near the village of Charlton Marshall. He worked there for almost a year. He was reasonably content there, although his only bed was in the barn and there was never enough food. He was always hungry but in truth he could not really remember feeling any other way. He had to leave there eventually because Marian, the farmer's sixteen year old daughter was becoming too fond of him, and he knew he did not love her enough to stay.

It was on the road after leaving the farm that he came upon Milton Abbey church and loved it so much. Two weeks later, hungry and exhausted, he called at a small farm and gained employment with the farmer's widow. He was pleasantly surprised at this turn of events, because the farm and cottage did not look prosperous enough to employ anyone. But Glenda Miles, the owner, seemed in no doubt that she wanted him to stay. She took him by the hand and drew him into the cosy cottage, seating him on the settle in front of the fire. She then prepared him the best meal he had seen for years. He fell asleep as soon as he had finished eating and did not awaken until the next morning.

(I had a funny thing happen regarding this memory. I had been telling a friend about this episode, and I had tried to picture Ryan fitting his

216

frame on to the narrow wooden settle and actually being able to sleep, cramped as he would have been on the hard surface. Instantly I heard Ryan's voice in my head, so clearly that I believe he must have said these exact words to me as Madeleine.

He said, 'I was so weary, I could have slept on the back of a hedge-pig with hitches.' I soon realised that this meant - I could have slept on the back of a hedgehog with hiccups - what a great saying!)

Glenda was a Welsh-woman by birth, a buxom lady, with laughing brown eyes, and long, curly flaxen hair. It was Glenda who elected to teach Ryan the arts of the bedchamber.

Ryan slept each night on the settle whilst Glenda retired to the only bedchamber upstairs. On the Friday night Glenda allowed that after she had retired he might bathe in front of the fire in the tin bath. Ryan undressed and climbed into the bath. Sheer luxury - he could not remember the last time. He was busy lathering himself and did not realise straight away that Glenda had re-entered the room behind him. She stood there quietly for a few moments watching him. Finally he looked back and saw her there. She smiled at him and walked round to the front of the bath. She was naked. Ryan's eyes grew wide. He had never seen a naked woman and he had never seen such a wonderful sight. He had played games with young ladies and he had been excited by them, but he had not lain with one.

He did not know what he was to do or say, so he just stared. She stepped up to the bath, smiling once more at his stunned look. She had hoped that she was to be his first, and she could see that she was. Ryan swallowed, feeling more nervous than he had ever thought he would at that moment.

'I have never—' he began.

'Good,' she replied. 'That is even better.' She began to run her hands over him, the soapy water making her touch glide like silk. Then she began to stroke him. It was too much. With a loud moan, Ryan climaxed.

'I am sorry,' he gasped, thinking that she would be disappointed in him.

'It is all right,' she whispered. 'It will be easier now. Come with me.' She took his hand, and drew him, still soaking wet, upstairs to her bedchamber. There she bade him lie on her bed. He knew the theory of love-making, but he was concerned that he might make a mistake. He need not have been concerned…He knew without doubt that he would never forget this night, or this woman, as long as he lived.

Later when she had finally sated him enough so that his body's desire had waned, a new desire grew in him, a desire to please this woman as much as she had pleased him. And it was then that she began to educate him in how to explore her body's most intimate secrets. During that night, and every night for the following month, he became assured and confident, learning to control his own body and learning exactly where and when to touch her, to give her most pleasure.

When the month was over she announced to him that she was to be wed for the third time and that, though it saddened her, he would have to leave because her new husband's family would soon arrive to help her to move to London where he lived. So Ryan must go, before his presence was discovered. He left this latest home, and once more began to journey towards London, working wherever he could and eating whenever he could.

'When he came upon Madeleine for the first time,

she was lying on the ground, stunned from a blow to the head, having fallen from her horse. Two lads aged about fifteen were kneeling beside her, and Ryan saw with horror that they were not attempting to help her, as he had first supposed, but had lifted her skirts, and were trying, very roughly, to remove her undergarments. Anger swept over him and he launched himself bodily at one of them, knocking him over. Wasting not a second in his onslaught he grabbed the other lad by his collars and using his own body weight, dragged him sprawling. The first lad tried to grab him from behind but they were in truth both a pair of weaklings and Ryan easily shook him off. That they were also cowardly was evident from their attack on this defenceless lady, and it was no surprise when they both made off as soon as they could. Ryan hurried back to the lady, who was pulling her skirts down to cover herself. She scrambled away from him in panic and he realised that she had taken him for another villain.

'My lady,' he reassured her hurriedly, 'I would never hurt you. Indeed I have just seen off those who would have done you harm.'

Love was there for him also at first sight but he could tell from her clothes that she was high-born and could never be his. It was true that she took his part against her parents when they returned to her home, but that could have merely been her strong nature which, he soon learned, rebelled against restriction of any kind. She paid him a lot of attention in the following months but he did not dare hope. It would never be allowed.

When she came to his bed in the barn the first time, he was dumb-struck and a little horrified at the possible consequences, should she be discovered there. He pretended to be asleep but it became too

219

much. Her face when he suddenly opened his eyes was comical but so appealing. Before he knew it he had pulled her down to him and he was kissing her. It was a terrible mistake, he knew that immediately, and so he became more ardent, thinking to frighten her away. But it had not worked. He had felt her surrender, felt her body soften against his and realised it was all going too far. So he feigned rejection of her. It hurt him as much as it did her but he knew not what else to do. Her parents would never allow him to be with her, and for the first time in many years he was not having to try and sleep every night with the pain of an empty belly.

He made sure they were never alone after that and he cruelly ignored her attempts to engage him in the sort of conversations he had loved before this unfortunate encounter. But then she had tricked him and he had openly showed his feelings for her. That night, when she came to him once more in the barn, he had tried so hard to resist those feelings, but the truth surfaced insistently, like larva from a volcano. He had tried not to touch her, to look at her, but he had struggled in vain. Then once more she was in his arms, soft and yielding. She had read the love in his eyes that was plain to see and he could resist no more. He knew he could have bedded her there and then but now that he had admitted his love he had to be more circumspect than ever. If her parents discovered this love they would be furious, so at least he must maintain her honour and give her parents nothing to use against them. But it became so difficult. Beneath the rug he was naked and his body was almost painfully aroused by the feel of her bare arms on his chest, by the soft weight of her. Fortunately for them both, Madeleine at last recognised that she must leave and did so. He had not known that she was seen leaving the barn until it became obvious from her father's visit, and the offer of a bribe. Ryan was so tired of wealthy people. All his life he had watched while they heartlessly bought everything with their riches, sometimes even poor peoples' souls. His own soul was not for sale. By offering him this bribe they made it easier for him. For once he was going to follow his heart, no matter what trouble it led him into, and they, for all their finery, would not stop him.

He had not expected Madeleine's parents to act so quickly on their threat to his person, and he was to pay for that mistake.

He had been sent to Hambledon village to collect a new iron gate from the smithy and his carrying this unwieldy object was what had helped the men to surprise him. He was taking his usual shortcut across the lane at the back of the village, and was so occupied with manhandling the gate over the hedge that he did not see the stealthy figures skulking in the shadows. The gate clanged to the ground and he bent to pick it up. That was when he saw movement out of the corner of his eye and he straightened hurriedly once more, stepping away from the gate to avoid being tripped by it should he need to move quickly. For he had a very unsettled feeling about the two men who were then approaching him.

'Excuse me, good sir,' one spoke, his manner well out of keeping with his appearance. 'Is this the right road for Hambledon?'

If this enquiry was meant to put Ryan off his guard, it did not work. He took two steps back, ready to flee or fight as circumstances dictated. But the steps back were halted as he realised that two more men were behind him. Ryan turned to assess this new danger and the men stood there, grinning nastily. And worse yet, two more men emerged from the shadows. He was surrounded. Six of them now and every one looking like the spawn of the devil. Ryan's heart began to pound rapidly, though he gave no outward sign. He was sure they would be on him like a pack of wolves at the first sign of weakness. The men began to circle him, all pretence gone now.

'What is it that you want?' Ryan asked, his voice steady.

'Just a little entertainment,' said one.

'Of course,' another chuckled, 'you may not find it entertaining.'

>From the third, 'But we will earn our pay, just the same.'

'And we enjoy our work,' said the next.

'Take a great pride in a job well done,' came from the fifth man.

The sixth man said nothing but stepped forwards and shoved Ryan in the chest, trying to unbalance him. But Ryan was planted like a tree, and did not move.

The sixth man spoke, 'Now give us no trouble and it will be over quickly. The end is inevitable, for any hurt you inflict on us will only serve you worse in the end. Give us trouble, and we will enjoy our work all the more, for we have plenty of time.' He laughed, and the others laughed too.

Ryan swallowed. His mouth was dry, and a sour taste filled his throat. He had faced this kind of threat before but not against six. He knew that one way or another he was going to be badly hurt and the knowledge was very unpleasant. At that moment Madeleine rushed into the lane. That made things even worse, for he could not hope to protect her against six. He had tried to make her leave, but she was as stubborn as always and would not go. When she attacked one of the men, employing her banshee scream, he was not surprised for he had seen that fire in her eyes before. Anticipating her in fact, he smacked a fist into one man's face and that man dropped to the ground as if pole-axed. Madeleine had felled her man too with a hefty blow from a solid branch. But now the men divided their attention. Two ran at Madeleine and two at him. His dismay at this attack on Madeleine, lent fury to his strength and, wanting to help her, he quickly threw one of his attackers to the ground, bloodied.

A well-aimed kick knocked the second man down, and Ryan's fist was already swinging towards his face when the shout of 'Stop!', came from the men's leader. Madeleine tried to tell him that she would not be harmed but the other men were already scrambling to their feet and Ryan knew his chance was gone. Besides the sight of the two ruffians hands on her conjured up visions too awful to chance. So he stopped, letting his hands fall limply to his sides. Two men continued to hold Madeleine fast as she screamed and fought while the two men Ryan had felled pounced on him vengefully.

His fists clenched once more, involuntarily, his arm muscles tensing as the men took hold of him. Obviously feeling the potential there for further harm to themselves, the men twisted his arms behind his back, their fingers digging fiercely into the skin of his forearms as they tightened their grip to forestall any resistance. But he dare not resist, lest they harm Madeleine. He refused to show any pain as they twisted his arms and he tried not to show his fear either, although only a fool would not feel that fear. A third man got to his feet and cockily strutted up to him. Ryan sneered in his face, though his chest was tight and his stomach knotted. The first punch felt like a hammer blow to his ribs, and Ryan grunted as the wind was knocked out of him. Then the man hit him in the mouth, and he tasted salty blood. Soon he could not breathe for the blows to his body, and soon everything went black.

He was dragged unwillingly from this darkness by a sudden excruciating pain in his back. Light seeped into his eyes and he realised he was lying on the road, dust in his mouth, and that he had been kicked. A hand snatched at his hair and pulled his head up. Foul breath puffed into his face and a voice heard through a dizzying fog said, 'Last chance lad. Will you swear to leave this place and never return?'

His mouth felt swollen and unresponsive but Ryan managed to utter, 'No…I will not,' knowing that it would bring further punishment but unable to deny himself.

The men seemed pleased to be refused this way; they laughed and began to kick him again, each one eager for his turn. Ryan twisted and turned on the ground but was unable to avoid the blows. Instinct drove him to his hands and knees but a kick to his abdomen tossed him over on his side once more. The men began to taunt him. They became excited and out of control.

'Come on then!—Get up!—Get up!' they yelled at him. 'Crawl!—Crawl!—On your belly!' He did try to get up again, something drove him to keep trying. But it was useless. The men ran around, competing for the best position to kick him again. Ryan was gasping for breath, as again and again he was winded by a kick and his strength was fading fast. His body was almost numb to the pain by now but he felt terribly sick and weak. He saw the final blow coming and he tried to avoid it, but the boot hit him squarely between his legs and the worst pain he had ever known blazed through his entire body, so that he cried out in agony. The rest was nothing compared to this. It was as if every nerve-ending in his body was centred in his groin and a wave of nausea overwhelmed him. He curled up reflexively, gasping and retching.

The man leaned down and said the words, 'Now you will choose to leave!'

Ryan had no answer, for he could not speak.

He saw their feet retreating and then Madeleine was there beside him. Still he could not speak and torrents of pain clouded his mind. Madeleine was distraught, crying out his name. In response, he tried to get up but the pain took his strength and his legs would not obey him. Madeleine took his arm and tried to pull him up, but he could not bear to be moved. He found his voice now and begged her to leave him alone. He did not know how long it might be until he could bear to move but for now he just needed to be still, for every muscle twitch sent fresh bolts of pain rippling through him. Finally she left him, and eventually came back with two workmen. They tried to be careful, but the journey back to the barn was a seemingly unending haze of hurting. When they lay him on the straw, he was pathetically grateful, just for the cessation of movement.

Nancy helped him though it was hard to let her. It was better when she sent Madeleine away for he could not bear the anguish on her face. At last the pain eased to a level that was bearable but at any threat of movement his protesting torn muscles and bruised innards shattered him with terrible cramps. It was a very long night.

It seemed that Madeleine's dire warning to her parents stopped them from any further violent act against him but he always knew that he lived under threat from that time. He had many, many, happy times with Madeleine and he would never have left her, but he knew in his heart that sooner or later her parents would succeed in getting rid of him for good. He lived for the moment, for the day, for he knew that was all he could be sure of.

Ryan did try and persuade Madeleine to leave on a few occasions, but truly it was only in a half-hearted way - for he already carried the guilt of being unable to provide for his sisters. Times were very hard and he was penniless. He could not bear the thought of Madeleine one day sharing the fate of his sisters. At least while they remained at the house she would never want for food or shelter.

(I found Ryan's perception of Madeleine very touching. It also gave me new insight into my character in this present life.)

Ryan thought she brought light into his life - light that had been sadly lacking for the most part. He loved her with so much of his heart that it was almost frightening. He knew that to love someone more than yourself was so dangerous but, once found, that kind of love could never be let go. Madeleine's love for him was transparent for all to see. She showed it in her every look and gesture. As regards their love-making, it was clear to him that she saw his erections as the ultimate magic trick and she always sought new and exciting ways to call upon this magic. He had been her teacher but she was soon on equal terms with him in her knowledge, for once he had overcome her initial shyness she was an avid student. She loved to play games and drew him into them, banishing his usual seriousness for a while.

He knew with a dreadful certainty that bad times would eventually come, the odds against them were too great for it to end any other way. But the love they shared was so special that it was worth the cost, whatever that cost turned out to be. He put all thoughts of the future aside. One time he remembered fondly was an occasion when he and Madeleine spent the whole night outdoors. He had done it many times out of necessity but she of course had not. They spent the afternoon collecting firewood and making a shelter out of poles and leafy branches lest the weather should turn bad. But it was a beautiful night. There was only a tiny crescent moon so that the stars were dazzling, both in their brilliance and their number. Poets through the ages had written of beauty beheld in the moonlight, but to Ryan's eyes nothing would ever compare to the sight of Madeleine, as she came to him, naked under the crystal light of a million stars - and then as she walked into the warm orange glow of the fire. She took his breath away. The dancing light rippled over her body, creating dark valleys and graceful peaks. Her hair glistened as if it too were afire. As always, just the touch of his mouth on hers excited them both and brought forth the magic she so loved - instantly. Ryan was still fully clothed but she reached down and a satisfied smile grew on her face as she felt his hardness, the immediate reaction delighting her. Then she undressed him, taking her time, caressing each part of him as it was uncovered. By the time he was naked he could hardly wait to join with her. He lifted her up till she could wrap her legs around his waist and he carried her this way, over to a broad tree. Leaning her back against it, while keeping his arms around her to protect her skin from the rough bark, he entered her in a single thrust. This was a quick coupling, what they both wanted this time.

227

Later he took more time, caressing her in ways he knew would bring her most pleasure - she so much bolder now than she was in the beginning.

Finally they lay in contented exhaustion, side by side, looking up at the stars and gradually drifting into a peaceful sleep. They awoke with the dawn and watched the sky turn. They saw first a faint yellow sliver that warmed through to peach, then finally to a pink and red fire, then the sky itself transformed from a watery blue to a deep cobalt. The birds serenaded them while they ate.

❧

When he was captured in the house it was truly his worst nightmare made real. Two of the men took a tight hold on his upper arms while the third put an arm around his throat from behind. It happened so quickly. Madeleine grasped his hands, which he could not move, and he only had hold of her fingers, so that when they were prised open, he had nothing to cling to.

(It has crossed my mind so many times, useless though it may be, that if only, as Madeleine, I had waited a moment and let Ryan get a firm grip on my wrists instead of clutching at his fingers, then with his strength we may have resisted their attempts to pull us apart. But as I always did then, and still do now, I rushed ahead impulsively, and gave him no chance to use his advantage. Maybe if we'd had a few more seconds, Ryan may have been able to do something.)

Distressed by Madeleine's desperate cries, Ryan struggled but was pulled backwards out into the hall, choking at the pressure on his throat. Once out there he managed to twist in their grasp and fight back. He was outnumbered of course, three to one. With hindsight he wished that he had given in at this point. Maybe had he been conscious on the way to the docks an opportunity for escape may have presented itself. However he could still hear Madeleine's cries and instinct took over. He managed to elicit several yelps of pain from his attackers until one resorted to the cudgel and a blow to Ryan's head knocked him senseless.

When he came to he was bound hand and foot on the bunk in a small cabin in the bow of the ship. Fortunately he did not suffer from sickness at the sea's motion for he was left that way until the ship was well out to sea. (It must have been awful for someone with a fear of drowning to be held helpless this way. If the ship had struck trouble - he would have been unable to try and save himself at all.) When he was finally released from his bonds he was allowed on deck, but he was chained like an animal by one ankle to a hatchway. He learned that it was no use to rant and struggle, for if he did then two of the sailors would unceremoniously toss him through the hatch, to land heavily down below. Then the hatch would be slammed shut for several hours until they decided to release him again.

When they finally disembarked for the first time Ryan had no idea where he was. He discovered that he was not the only unwilling participant on this journey. At the training camp there were six others who were kept in chains, night and day. Ryan had never held a broadsword but fairly quickly developed the skill to use it. Fortunately for him he was blessed with strong arms and legs and the kind of stamina which could cope with the tough training regime. Some of the other prisoners were not so blessed and he saw two die in the course of training, not strong enough to carry the heavy sword well enough to defend themselves. He was constantly watched, and escape seemed impossible.

Ryan only had one chance when it seemed worth trying to escape. It looked too good to be true at first. His leg shackle was worn and rusty and he spent many hours after dark trying to break it open, but, alas, it did not appear to be weak enough for that. However, one afternoon when he was re-chained to his cot after a training session, he distinctly heard a snap as the key was turned. He coughed quickly, to cover the sound, praying that the guard had not heard it. His prayers were answered. This guard's attitude to him had mellowed over the weeks of training. He had gained some respect for Ryan, because of his fast developing skill. Maybe that was the reason why he did not tug at the shackle to test it. As soon as he was out of sight, Ryan pulled at the shackle and it sprang open. The pin that turned the lock had sheered away and the lock was useless. He pushed it closed again and waited impatiently for nightfall, dreading the possibility of discovery every time anyone came near. He waited until the camp was quiet, and there was only he and one other prisoner in the tent. Sadly it was this other prisoner that caused Ryan's downfall.

When this other prisoner saw Ryan remove his broken shackle and stand up he began demanding to go too. There was nothing Ryan could do for him, for he had no key and the other man's shackle was still locked tight. But the man would not, could not, I suppose, accept it, and he threatened to raise the alarm if Ryan did not help him escape too.

'But there is no way I can help you,' Ryan protested. 'What can I do?'

'Go you and steal the keys,' the prisoner insisted.

But Ryan knew this would be a fool's errand, as the keys were worn at night on the belt of the commanding officer. There was no way he could get them, at least not without being both willing and able to kill several armed men. He sat back down with a sigh, deciding to postpone his escape bid until this other man was asleep or his conscience made him let Ryan go in silence.

But the man was more desperate than Ryan knew (in fact he was one of those that was to die in training), and seeing that his ploy had failed, he began to shout the alarm anyway. Perhaps he thought he could win favour for himself by betraying his fellow prisoner. Ryan had to make a quick decision, run and risk almost certain capture, suffering whatever punishment was seen as fit for such an attempt or be found with the broken shackle, and be punished in any case. In a split second he made the decision to run. He got to his feet and dived under the back wall of the tent. The other prisoner must have had a conscience after all for now he fell silent. Everything seemed to snag at Ryan's clothes, conspiring to delay him - first the tent, then the brambles outside. Still, in seconds he was clear of them and up and running as fast as he could, away from the camp. But the night-watch, alerted by the shouts, was already riding around the perimeter of the camp in anticipation. They were bearing down on him as soon as he cleared the bushes. He had no chance. They overtook him and turned their mounts sharply, cutting him off. Ryan felt almost insane at that moment. He was furious with the other prisoner, with fate, with God. That was why he did not do the sensible thing and surrender. He angrily grabbed the leg of one of the mounted soldiers and yanked him from his horse. But these were professional soldiers and, before he could attempt to get on the horse, others were upon him from behind. Several pairs of hands caught hold of him, and sheer weight of numbers bore him to the ground. When he had finally ceased his futile struggling, they dragged him to his feet and marched him back into the centre of the camp.

This time he was shackled firmly by his wrists to the punishment pole in the middle of the training compound and left there until morning. At that time the whole company turned out for their drills and the normal business of the morning began around him. At noon two soldiers came to Ryan where he sat and pulled him to his feet. The chain holding his captive hands was detached from its low ring, and locked into a higher one which pulled his arms up over his head. Ryan felt a cold knot of fear in his stomach - so he was to be treated as a deserter. He had seen this punishment inflicted before and he knew only too well what was to happen to him.

One of the officers approached him, carrying an evil-looking leather-thonged whip which he handed to one of the soldiers. 'Ten,' he said to the soldier. He came up close to Ryan and said to him quietly, 'Foolish lad. You were doing so well but I have to show an example. Be strong - bite down on this.' He placed a piece of hard wood between Ryan's teeth.

Then the lash whistled through the air and Ryan gripped the piece of wood tight with his teeth, determined not to cry out. But when the lash struck and cut into his shoulders he was stunned by the sharpness of the pain. He struggled to restrain the groan that forced itself past his clenched teeth. His eyes opened wide with the shock of it. The whip cracked nine more times until his legs felt weak and his knees tried to buckle under him. Desperately, he strove to stay on his feet while he was unchained and led back to his bunk. His dignity in front of the other men was all he had left now. (You know this is very distressing for me to commit to paper. I can hardly bear the thought that Ryan went through this all alone. It was so unfair. When I finally talk to Garth about all this it may make him understand why he is so apparently lucky in his present life - for he doesn't seem to believe he deserves it - you and I know differently.)

He was left on his own in the tent, once more shackled but this time with bright new chains. He knew that if he were left unattended then the worst of his pain was to come. He could feel thin trickles of blood running down his back and this blood would dry, sticking his shirt to the wounds. And his back would stiffen badly. Already the slightest movement of his shoulders burned fiery strands into his skin. He sat, head bowed, his arms resting on his knees, hands dangling. He felt desperately unhappy, desperately alone and desperately heartsick. He longed for Madeleine to hold him. The thought that he might never see her or touch her again filled him with dark despair. He often dreamed of her, only to awaken to the realisation that it was just a dream and that for him reality was a cold and lonely place. His courage did not often fail him but now he had truly had enough. What he needed above all else was to be held and comforted in the arms of someone who loved him. He felt the prickle of self-pitying tears behind his eyes and he squeezed them away, angrily.

The same officer who had given Ryan the piece of wood came into the tent. Ryan looked sideways up at him from where he sat on the edge of his cot.

Seeing his facial expression, the officer seemingly felt some pity. 'I'll get you some help,' he said, and withdrew.

This officer seemed like a decent man and Ryan wondered what lies he had been told about his prisoners in order that his conscience would permit this brutal treatment of them. A few minutes later a plump, matronly woman appeared. She was carrying a pail of water, some rags and a jar of salve. Ryan recognised her as being one of the army's washer-women. She clucked in disapproval at the sight of him but wasted no time.

'Lay you down, my lad,' she ordered briskly, her red, work-weary hands taking hold of him and guiding him face down on the cot. 'I will see you to rights.' Despite the roughness of her hands, she lifted his shirt very gently and pulled it up in order to reach the wounds. His shirt was ragged for it had been torn by the whip in the same way as his skin. When she began to dab at the cuts with a wet rag Ryan could not help but flinch from the sting, drawing his breath in sharply, his hands closing into tight fists. But soon the cool water began to soothe and he was grateful for it. When the wounds were clean she carefully patted his back dry. Then she used her leathery hands to smooth the healing salve over each weal.

'That is done, lad,' she stood up. 'You will be mended in a few days.'

He sighed with relief and sagged against the mattress. 'Thank you,' he said, 'You are a good woman.'

When she had left, however, he became maudlin again for the woman reminded him of Nancy and her kind ministerings, and he wished with all his heart that he could change his fate.

The next day lifting the broadsword was a torture.

Two days after this dispiriting event a worse fate befell the prisoner who had betrayed Ryan. This man had never mastered the broadsword, for wielding the heavy weapon and the equally heavy shield were beyond his power; he already bore several cuts and bruises sustained during his training. Ryan felt some sympathy for him now because he too was in discomfort from the stiffness of his wounds, and he realised that this man had borne that kind of pain all along. His arms were probably aching unbearably from the strain. Ryan at least had his strength though it hurt now to use it. This other prisoner (Ryan never knew his name), was slightly built and, as he was only just over five feet three inches tall, his reach was also lacking. Ryan could no longer find it in his heart to blame the man for trying any avenue to gain an advantage.

This morning there was an urgency in the air. It seemed that the battle they were being trained for was fast approaching. Parts of the encampment had been packed up ready for transportation back to the ship. The training of late had become more frantic. Now this other prisoner was being harried mercilessly. He had not made the grade and therefore had become expendable. He was being pushed to his limit and beyond, in an attempt to find some improvement in his skills. Ryan was about fifty paces from him when the real trouble began. It was obvious that the soldiers had lost all patience with the unfortunate man. And the soldier he was sparring with lunged forward, totally serious, not holding back. The prisoner's sword clattered to the stony ground as a jarring blow spun it from his hands. His courage deserted him and he backed away from his assailant, hands upraised in mute surrender. To Ryan's horror, the soldier ignored this gesture and pressed his attack. The prisoner staggered and ran as the soldier's sword slashed at him, barely missing. He began a stumbling run towards Ryan. Perhaps his fevered mind hoped for help there. Sheer terror masked the man's face but Ryan could do nothing; he was unarmed and anyway too far away. Nevertheless he ran towards the man, unable to ignore the tortured plea expressed by the rigid grimace on his face. They were still ten paces apart when the broadsword sliced through the air once more, this time finding its target as it struck the man on the back of his neck, almost severing his head from his shoulders. His still flailing body pitched forwards and fell onto Ryan. He caught the man in his arms, blood pouring over his hands and sleeves. Gasping in horror, he lowered him to the ground. The man's eyes were glazed over, empty and lifeless. Ryan looked up at the soldier, grief and anger plain in his eyes. He stood up quickly, wiping his bloody hands on his breeches and glowered at the soldier.

'Why?' he asked. 'Why do this?'

The soldier shrugged. It was obvious that this life he had snuffed out meant no more to him than if he had crushed an insect beneath his boot.

'He was useless—hopeless—a waste of effort. He would have slowed us down.'

Ryan stepped forward threateningly. The soldier yelled, 'Back off!' and raised his sword. Ryan did not move, his eyes glittering with disgust at this disregard for a human life.

The soldier lifted his sword and pressed the point against Ryan's throat, saying, 'I said—back off!'

At this moment an officer who had been watching intervened, placing his hand on the sword.

236

'No,' he said to the soldier, 'this one is a good swordsman, we will need him. Leave him to me.'

The soldier let the point of his sword drop to the ground and then, with a sneer, he turned and walked away. Ryan looked down once more at the body at his feet, trying to calm the rage he felt at this senseless slaughter. Finally he looked at the officer. 'For the love of God—why?' he asked. 'Why not just let him go if he was of no use to you?'

'None of you can ever be released,' the officer replied. 'Those are our orders.'

So Ryan knew now for sure that, no matter what he did, no matter how hard he fought for the King, he was never to be released and never to see Madeleine again. His thoughts turned inwards and he gazed at the officer with unseeing eyes, struggling to accept his fate. The officer walked away, not wanting to provoke Ryan into rash action for he knew that he would need all the strong sword arms he could muster.

As I had thought, they did make shore the second time at Sunderland. At this point, Ryan and the other prisoners had been shackled to each other in the middle of the small column to prevent escape and they had of course been given no weapons. When they were suddenly attacked by the English deserters, both officers were killed and a lot of the men. The Englishmen did not seem eager to stay long - perhaps they knew that the Scottish army was nearby. They seemed mainly to want to take as many weapons as they could which left Ryan's band almost defenceless. By now Ryan had no choice but to stay with the others. A lot of them were wounded and there were only about twenty on their feet. Four of these had been prisoners like himself.

They decided to head back to the ship. But, as you and I know, they did not make it. It amazed me when I realised that through all this time Ryan too felt a vestige of guilt that he had not forced Madeleine to leave with him - so he did know he could have done if he had really tried. I wonder then if Garth has the same problem that I do - a feeling of not deserving the wonderful wife he has, the beautiful children and, of course, his success. He won't understand, I doubt, if I ever get a chance to say to him quietly, 'Madeleine never blamed you - she only blamed herself.' It might make a difference to him, though, because his deep subconscious will understand.

Ryan felt guilty that he had not managed to escape though it's hard to see how he could have done. After the skirmish with the English, he did start to harbour hopes of escaping in the ship and sailing back to Madeleine. He was filled with horror at what would happen to her if she were left alone. He knew she could never survive without him. It was a burden he had always carried. But when the Scottish army attacked he knew he would not survive. One look at their faces was enough. They were not going to leave anyone alive. What went through his mind as he was so brutally slain?

After the initial agony of the strikes - a cold numbing pain that slowly turned unbearably hot - he did indeed retreat to a dream world. This was a dream world that had often saved his sanity in the past, during the many tough episodes of his life. He saw his mother for a while though she was long dead before he left Ireland. Then his thoughts turned back to Madeleine. His last thoughts were of her. At one point he even thought he could see her bending over him with deep concern. And he thought her hand reached out and touched him. His last thought, however, was one of despair as to how she would take the news of his death.

I think that this dying moment of panic was what caused Ryan's soul to delay its onward journey, in order to go back for her and take her out of a world that she could never remain sane in. If our purpose in this world is to learn unconditional love then I believe, of all people, Ryan and Madeleine truly did.

❧

I found it hard to end the ceremony. I had to find something truly special to say - from me. This is what I came up with.

'Madeleine, you have been a secret part of me for over three hundred years. You have been standing in the wings, waiting for a chance to tell your tragic tale. I'm sorry it took me so long. Now I know you, I welcome you with an open heart into my present life. You can rest now, your job is done. I know you will still need to see Ryan and I will try everything in my power to make it happen. Welcome home.'

'Ryan, as Madeleine I have loved you through all time. I still love you. For that part of me that will always be Madeleine, I will try and establish contact with you. For even if you never remember, and never recognise her, she needs to be able to see you. I am sorry, so sorry, for all you had to go through for Madeleine. Be happy and free. Goodbye, my love.'

Chapter Twenty

It finally came to me that I already knew the reason for my fear of the knife-grinder whom I saw at the market during that very vivid regression.

I'd had a very unforgettable nightmare concerning this man years previously. Now I remembered it again, for it was the kind of nightmare that lives with you forever; then everything fell into place. I know now that I have had memories of this past life before, and probably others too. I don't know exactly when this event took place, but it was after the harvest fair, so Madeleine's fear of him must have been by way of premonition.

'When Ryan was working out in the far fields, I did not usually venture out to meet him, more often waiting for him at the bridge - for it was a far distance from the house and a long way to walk alone, and unprotected. However on this occasion it was my intention to do so for I had been missing Ryan's presence a great deal this day and I could not wait patiently for his return.

'So I had crossed the brook by way of the footbridge and I was making my way, deep in thought, through the woodland which marked the boundary between the farm fields and the outlying estate. I hardly saw the trees as they thickened or the grass underfoot, as my mind dwelt solely on Ryan. I knew that he would be surprised and delighted at my unexpected arrival. My reverie was snatched from me, however, as my senses began to detect stealthy sounds and pulled my attention to them. I could hear what sounded like almost an echo of my own movements. But when I paused suddenly I could still hear this echo. Someone was following me. It need not mean danger, I tried to tell myself. Maybe some innocent traveller was merely coincidentally following my path. But my heart thudded and a tingle of fear invaded my blood for I knew without doubt that there was danger.

'I resumed walking, instinct telling me not to let my tracker know that I had detected him. If he intended to attack me that might force his hand. But if he felt that his presence was yet undetected, maybe I could get to Ryan and safety. Indeed I now realised that I was only forty paces from the edge of the trees. From there I would be able to call to Ryan and he might even see me, depending on which field he had been working in; for by this hour he should be making his way towards me. I considered whether I should call out now in the hope that Ryan might already be able to hear me. But if he could not and I warned my stalker that I knew of his presence, then all would be lost. Another choice would be to run but the man, whoever he was, was close behind, and would no doubt catch me before I could reach safety. I began to wish I had not been so foolish as to come here alone.

'Suddenly all my choices were gone. A hand gripped my gown from behind and another grasped my hair. I was pulled backwards and before I could make any sound apart from a sharp cry of shock, the hand released my gown and clamped instead my mouth. When I hit the ground the wind was knocked from me. I gasped for breath as the man launched himself bodily on top of me. But then I let out a breathy scream, for I recognised the man as the knife-grinder from the fair. I was able to utter this scream because the hand that had masked my mouth now grasped my right wrist in an effort to hold me still. I was sickened, both by the obvious threat and by his close proximity to me. His face above mine, was red and fevered as his animal cravings drove him. His hair hung in greasy ribbons around his head and his breath smelled noxious with stale beer. He held my head pinned to the ground by his grip on my hair but my left hand was free. I began to hit at him with this free hand but my blows were feeble and weak with dread. He did not speak but dodged my blows easily, his breathing fast and frenzied. Up close I could see his pale blue eyes, the whites an unhealthy yellow, bulging against his purplish complexion and I could see the veins standing out on his brow. I could see the stubble of his unshaven beard where it folded into the creases and valleys of his pock-marked skin. He let go of my hair, using his body weight to hold me down and with total horror I felt him begin to scrabble at my skirts. I twisted and fought, but then I could feel his fingernails scraping against the bare skin of my legs. I convulsed with abhorrence and now I really screamed but this time one word, 'Ryan!', over and over again. I felt the man's posture stiffen as I cried out and I suspect he knew for whom I was calling, and perhaps had not expected him to be near.

'To my unending relief I heard a cry in the distance and I recognised Ryan's voice. This lent me

242

new strength and I writhed violently in the man's grasp, reaching for his eyes with my free hand, the fingers curling into talons. I raked his cheek as he tried to dodge my attack. It was suddenly all too much for him; his face was bleeding and he must have known that Ryan was coming - and coming fast. He scrambled up and made off through the trees.

'I sat up shakily. I was not damaged so I climbed to my feet and clung to a tree trunk to support my trembling legs. I thanked God he had not touched me in a more intimate way, else I would never have washed his filth from myself. I heard someone crashing through the trees and Ryan's frantic voice calling out my name. I answered him, guiding him to me. At the sight of him I almost collapsed with relief. He too looked most thankful that I appeared to be safe. He rushed to me and swept me into his embrace, filling me with a safe warm feeling which banished all fear.

'"What has happened?" he asked anxiously.

'I replied, my mouth close to his ear as he held me, "It was the knife-grinder from the fair, he—he—" I hesitated, fearing Ryan's reaction which I knew would be ferocious. If I said too much too quickly Ryan would kill the man and I had no desire for a death to darken my love's soul. "I—I am not harmed," I reassured him, "merely shaken."

'"What did he do?" Ryan demanded.

'"He came upon me from behind, forced me to the ground—" It was enough. Ryan went rigid with fury.

'"Which direction did he take?" he asked in a voice that was as hard as iron and yet as brittle as glass.

'"I do not know, perhaps towards the village— but Ryan—"

'"Yes?" he said. I could see that he was torn between the need to pursue and run down this foul villain and the need to stay with me and be my protector.

'"Please. Do not leave me. Let God see that he is punished. I am still afraid and I need you to hold me." I could see that he was still tempted to set off on a journey of revenge so I continued to persuade, clinging tightly to him, feeling coiled springs beneath his shirt. "He may come back if you leave me. I cannot be sure which path he took. He may still be nearby, waiting for you to leave. Please my love, please, take me home."

'Reluctantly he agreed, and with his arm tight about me we set off. I realised at this moment how safe I had felt since Ryan had come into my life and I thanked God for his presence there with me. I also thanked God later that Ryan did not find the knife-grinder. Here was one trader, I felt, who would not be appearing at next year's fair.'

❦

The nightmare that I had suffered previously concerned the part where this revolting character and I (as Madeleine) struggled on the ground. I will never forget his face or the awful feeling of powerlessness his attack caused in me. We all like to think that, were we attacked in this way, we would fight furiously - but my muscles became as weak as water and I could not seem to hit him with any strength at all. I am, though, quite relieved to discover the source of this nightmare for I had feared that it was a premonition of an attack to come but now I know it is in the past.

It is difficult in these enlightened times to imagine that the well-bred women of that era went to their marriage beds, for the most part completely ignorant not only of how their own bodies worked but also about how a man's body was meant to work with it.

The men were often more experienced than the women but still totally ignorant, and usually uncaring, of a woman's needs. This meant that the wedding night was little more than legalised rape.

Nancy and her sister, Sarah, did their best to warn Madeleine of what she might expect but without being willing to come right out with it. It was all hint and innuendo which just completely confused her in her innocence. The conversation happened this way.

'The night before Ryan and I were to leave to be wed in secret I could not sleep, so knowing that Nancy's kind sister, Sarah, was visiting her, I sought these two good companions out. They were the only ones privy to the event, and so they were the only ones I could turn to. These two women were found, as I had thought, warming themselves in front of the kitchen fire with a goblet of wine. The big fire was now all cosy embers, turning the whole room into a comforting pink cave. After a while the conversation took a puzzling turn. With a knowing wink at Nancy, Sarah commenced.

'"Beware, my lady, of a well-endowed man for he may be impatient with you and thus cause you a great deal of pain." What could she mean by this? I asked her. She turned a little pink in the cheeks and her reply confused me even more.

'"Well, he may not be caring of your sensibilities. He may force his way with you and you may not be able to accommodate him without discomfort."

'I did not understand at all. Was she referring to his wealth or his property when she spoke of a man being well-endowed? In any case I knew this did not apply, for Ryan had neither wealth nor property. When I pointed this out they both showed signs of great mirth and laughed at me until I became quite angry.

'Finally Nancy patted my knee in an attempt to pacify me. "Do not concern yourself, my lady," she advised. "Ryan is a gentle and considerate man, and I know he will take good care not to hurt you, and he will, I am sure, see to it that you are made - content." This time it was she who winked at Sarah, and once more they were both consumed with laughter at my expense.

I decided to ignore their silliness. I could not imagine Ryan ever hurting me in any way and so I decided it was but a foolish jape on their part. I was intending to return to my bed but, almost without thinking, I found myself standing outside the barn doors. I opened one just a tiny crack, enough to see through. I resolved not to waken Ryan if he were asleep. He was not. He was sitting up in his makeshift bed, his knees bent in front of him, arms resting on them on top of the rug that covered him. He was chewing a piece of straw and it was quite plain that he had been expecting me to come. He patted the place at his side, inviting me to join him. When I reached his side I was surprised to see a second rug laid out next to his, in anticipation of my arrival. We said nothing - no words were needed. I crawled under the rug he had put out for me and turned on my side to face him. He also lay down.

'I began to recount to him the curious conversation I had had with Sarah and Nancy. His mouth began to twitch in amusement too, though he tried hard to hide it. He took in my totally puzzled and rather hurt expression and tried once more, but a broad grin forced itself onto his face. I felt quite upset that nobody would explain this matter to me in a way I could comprehend.

'He could see this so he said, "Do not worry, my love. You are right, I would never hurt you. They were just jesting with you. You will never have anything to fear from me. I will explain it all to you when we are wed and you will understand." But he was still smiling as he reached out and took my hand in his. Then we lay this way, only our eyes locked in an embrace until they finally closed in sleep.

'The first thing I saw when I awoke in the morning was Ryan's eyes regarding me. I knew at that very moment that the thing I most longed for in all the world was to awaken to this sight every day for the rest of my life.'

Chapter Twenty-one

The rest, as they say, is history. We joined this tale near the end, as now we leave it near the beginning.

Some friends have questioned why I have been shown these memories in such a strange order, starting at the end, so to speak, instead of at the beginning. This is quite simple to explain. It was terrible enough being shown how Ryan died while I only had my first inklings of remembering him. Had I been allowed to re-know him thoroughly as a person, and then been shown his death for the first time, it would have been unbearable. Once I had remembered what a truly exceptional and wonderful person he was and how much I had loved him, accepting his death now would have been almost as bad for me as it was then, for Madeleine.

Here is my own insight into their two characters. It has taken me some while to understand them both.

Ryan was intelligent and honest, sometimes a little intense. He was brave, loyal and passionate. He was very demanding on himself when it came to his sense of duty, and he expected equal integrity from others, always being very disappointed when he didn't get it. He had to grow up very fast, because his life became too serious too quickly. He never really had a childhood. He was very compassionate, and easily emotionally involved with anything he cared about. He had a temper that could be quickly aroused when he saw the injustices that the world inflicted on others, especially the poor and defenceless. His intellect was very important to him, as is evidenced by the fact that he could read and write, not a common talent given his background. He had gone to great pains as a young boy to ensure that he was taught, always encouraged by his mother, often riding through the night to reach whomever had agreed to teach him.

Madeleine was mischievous, sensual, and a little over-confident at times. When she loved, she loved with every part of her being, with nothing held back. She was totally loyal to Ryan and would have attacked anyone who tried to harm him. If only she had realised the real danger from her parents. In this she was a little naïve and childlike. She was brave, both for and with Ryan, but totally lost without him. She was not as proficient at reading and writing as he, but she had a poetic soul and she greatly appreciated his writings, and his eloquence.

Chapter Twenty-two

The only person we have not heard from yet is Nancy. She knew Ryan and Madeleine better than anyone else. I would love to rediscover this warm and caring person in my present life. She/he would certainly be a kindred spirit of mine. Maybe Garth knows her. Maybe there is someone in his life who has always stood behind him, protecting him, while keeping in the background. I have meditated, asking to know Nancy's thoughts, and this is what I have found out.

She was very pleased when Ryan appeared on the scene. She had been worried that Margaret would succeed in wasting Madeleine's young life, by marrying her off to a rich old man, and that she would therefore miss out on the chance of real love. Nancy had known love with her late husband. He had been a plain and poor man but he had loved her. She wanted Madeleine to know that kind of love. And then one day this young Irishman had walked into the kitchen and Nancy had thought straight away - this is the one for Madeleine. Nancy and her husband had known love but Ryan and Madeleine were different again. As their love grew it was as if their two souls had locked together forever, to form a greater whole than the sum of their two parts. When they were together they became so alive, and their happiness was so tangible that it seemed as if one could touch it. This tall blue-eyed man, with his great maturity and obvious inner strength had stolen Nancy's heart too. She had felt a huge surge of maternal protectiveness towards him, and was very hurt on his behalf at every rejection he suffered from Margaret and Edwin. He had a really admirable temperament which they never seemed to appreciate. True, he also had a hot Irish temper but it was only aroused in the defence of others. He was a born champion of the hurt and the lowly, and he had the physical ability and the courage to be their protector. Yet he could be so gentle, and so vulnerable.

Nancy could never understand why Margaret took against him so. He did stand in the way of her ambitions but Nancy had lost her heart to him the moment those stunningly blue eyes had met hers, so directly and so honestly; so, like Madeleine, she could not comprehend how anyone could fail to be captivated by him, let alone deliberately hurt him.

After Margaret had first tried bribery and then had him beaten, Nancy had been horrified. The woman's cruelty astounded and shocked her. And when Madeleine, almost hysterical with distress, had fetched her to the barn, she had been badly shaken to see the damage that had been inflicted on Ryan. He had been in terrible pain and the journey back to the barn, while well-meaning, had not helped at all.

Ryan had been lying curled up on his side, his hands fisted between his legs when Nancy had come in. And her first attempts to roll him onto his back had brought groans of protest from him and physical resistance to the movement. With Madeleine's help she had managed to get his shirt off. But the sight of the black and mottled skin of his abdomen and his constant, involuntary moans of pain had brought so much crying from Madeleine that Nancy had had to send her out. Nancy had been awfully aware that this blackness on his stomach indicated internal damage and could have spelt his death.

Once Madeleine had been persuaded that it would be better for Ryan if she left, Nancy had been able to be more forceful with him. And, despite his pleas to be left alone, she had managed to treat his injuries with healing herbal salves. She had allowed him to grip her hand so tightly that it had hurt her whenever his pain had become too much to bear alone. Fearful cramps had come over him and Nancy was glad that Madeleine did not witness the worst of these. Although Nancy had tried to keep herself tightly controlled, even she had not been able to stop large tears of sympathy from rolling down her cheeks.

At these bad moments, Nancy held him close, his face buried in her bosom, and she tried to soothe him with gentle words, 'Hush—hush my love—it will pass—it will pass. There is no justice in God's world, if they do not pay for this cruelty.'

He had not wanted her to remove his breeches, not wanting her to see him naked, but blood had seeped through and she really needed to assess and treat the damage. She found that the delicate skin there had been torn by the force of the boot. His mouth too had bled and was swollen. Nancy bathed both these areas with salt water to clean them, and had then applied the salve. Embarrassment at her necessary familiarity now put aside, Ryan was grateful for her gentle touch as the pain was eased.

When Ryan and Madeleine had confided in her their plans to be wed, Nancy was pleased. Like Madeleine she had hoped that Ryan would be accepted once it was done, and she had been greatly saddened when this had not been the case. It was incomprehensible to her that Margaret and Edwin would rather see their daughter married to some foppish, old, upper-class weakling than to this handsome young man, with his high principles, who was filled with a powerful life-force. What was money, compared to all this?

While, it was true, Ryan had already won Nancy's heart, the incident which really commanded her undying loyalty to him was something that Madeleine never even knew of. Nancy and Ryan had taken the pony and trap down to the village to collect haunches of venison from the annual cull and were coming back home with fully laden cart. They were passing the last cottage which lay on the right when they heard cries of distress. Ryan quickly reined the pony in and he and Nancy hurried around to the back of the cottage where the cries were coming from.

A frightening scene met their eyes. A small water tower in the back yard, built by the tenant, Graham Collinge, to save his family from having to fetch water from the village well every day, was collapsing. One of the three timber legs had been dislodged and was giving way, so that the water container on top was wobbling dangerously. The cries for help had come from Thomas Collinge. His sister, Sally, was only two years old, and had been playing under the tower. Her clothes had been snagged by some nails in the tower's damaged leg, and she was held fast. Meanwhile Thomas, who was eight years old and had been left in sole charge of his sister while his parents worked, was futilely trying to hold up the tower as it steadily bore down on his little sister. His efforts were, of course, in vain, and there were only seconds remaining before the infant was enveloped. As it fell the water would cascade out but that would not save her, for the barrel itself was more than heavy enough to crush her frail form.

Nancy and Ryan rushed forward in an instant, she to try and free the girl and he to try and stop the weight's descent. Sally could not be freed, because in her struggle she had twisted her dress tight around herself and strengthened the nails' grip on the cloth.

'I will need a knife!' Nancy shouted to Ryan as he threw his shoulder against the bottom of the barrel. Nancy came out from under the barrel and pulled Thomas with her to safety. 'Go into the house!' she ordered briskly. 'Fetch a knife, quickly!' She glanced at Ryan's face, seeing the grimace there as he strained against the weight, legs braced.

'Hurry!' she yelled at Thomas' retreating back. She turned back to Ryan, asking anxiously, 'Can you hold it?'

'Long—enough,' he grunted in reply.

All the same, Nancy grew ever more terrified as he staggered slightly, his legs shaking with the effort. As the barrel shifted several gallons of water poured down over him, making balance difficult while the container rocked. Nancy looked around at the back door; what was taking Thomas so long?

With an ominous creak the front leg fell out completely and crashed to the ground, inches from the crying child, its weight still enough to pin her there. Ryan groaned as the weight, bereft of even minimal support from the broken leg, became almost more than he could bear.

Nancy thought he could not possibly hold it and, not wanting both the child and Ryan to die, shouted, 'Let it go! You will have to let it go!'

Ryan did not answer but closed his eyes tightly, calling on some inner strength to help him, and he stood firm. Finally, Thomas re-emerged from the house, knife in hand, and Nancy snatched it from him. With a last look at Ryan's face for reassurance, she dived back under the threatening bulk of the barrel and slashed at the child's dress until she could tear her away to safety.

But then she realised that a problem still remained, for how was Ryan to escape? - for if he let go for an instant the barrel would crash to the ground around him. There was nothing to hand that could support the weight of the barrel.

'Ryan!' she called out in fear.

'Stand back!' he shouted.

When they were all a safe distance away, Ryan attempted what he had not dared while the infant was trapped beneath. He slowly bent his knees, relying for his life on the strength of his legs. They did not fail him. As he lowered the edge of the barrel, water began to torrent out, drenching him but steadily reducing the weight of the barrel. Then, as it began to disintegrate under the pressure of the water pouring out, Ryan was able to turn around and lower the almost empty container safely to the ground.

Nancy let out the terrified breath she had been holding in a whoosh and collapsed unceremoniously to the grass, the two children beside her. Ryan also fell to the ground next to her and all four sat, leaning against each other until their breathing calmed. After a while, Thomas began voicing a fear of chastisement from his parents, for he should never have allowed Sally to play near to the tower. Nancy and Ryan agreed not to tell anyone of the dreadful fate that almost befell Sally Collinge. Thomas, they felt, had learned his lesson.

Days later, Nancy was amazed that word of this brave deed had not even reached Madeleine's ears. She came to realise that Ryan saw the events differently to her. He did not consider what he had done as bravery. The fact was that God had endowed him with physical power, while as yet Thomas and Sally had none - so therefore it was only right that Ryan help them. Nancy came to understand then that he was so much deeper than most people realised.

Nancy had laughed at Madeleine's innocence on the night before she and Ryan left to get married. She was not truly worried about Madeleine's fate at Ryan's hands, for she knew from the servants' gossip that he was already an experienced and skilled bed-mate. Indeed, she knew that he had already been experienced when he came to ***** House. Since then two of the local female servants had enjoyed his intimate company and he was much sought after by them. But she also knew that he had not lain with another since declaring his love for Madeleine, keeping himself now only for her.

The day she had been attacked while out with the pony and trap, Nancy had had good reason to be so panic-stricken, for as a younger woman she had been raped at knife-point. These two robbers had brought all her submerged fear back to the surface. When she had almost fallen out of the trap in front of them, Ryan had known instinctively that she needed strong comfort, and she had sobbed with relief at his close presence and the feel of his arms around her. And when she had become hysterical again in the woods, from fear of the two men, he had been able to inspire great trust from her. Partly because of his impressive physical might and partly because she knew that he had risked his own life in order to protect others before. And so when he had sworn that he would not let the men harm her - she had believed him. And it had been true. He had stood his ground, shielding both her and Madeleine with his own body, and he had taken the cut from the knife in their defence without flinching.

Then there was the way that Ryan had handled Sarah's daughter, Emily, after she had been so brutally attacked. He had shown such wonderful sensitivity that it had been difficult to believe how young he was.

Again, Nancy puzzled over how Margaret could have remained so vindictive towards him. The woman had obviously been deranged. When he had been abducted, Nancy could not believe the terrible injustice of the world. What a waste, what a terrible, sinful, waste. She was almost as grief-stricken as Madeleine and she mourned with her. The poor child slowly lost her mind, as she could not bear having this man - who was part of her - taken so cruelly. Without him, she faded before Nancy's very eyes. When Madeleine took her own life, Nancy felt as if her own world had become unbearably empty, but she was glad that Madeleine was free from pain, for she never would have been had she continued to live.

Nancy was a good and loving soul, but she could not help but receive satisfaction from the final demise of Margaret.

Chapter Twenty-three

Finally, after what seemed like years of waiting, the day of the concert in Dublin loomed. After all the trauma, I was going to see Garth for real. The only remaining hurdle I had to get over was another ride on a plane. This time it would even be without the support of Tony, since we could not afford for both of us to go. However I was to go with a group of Garth's fans - so I knew I would be in good company. On this day I met some really great new friends. This is one of the big beneficial results of my experiences. I constantly find I am making new and rewarding contacts.

Anyway, I was certain that the trip would be worth a new scare or two. It was - it was even worth the three hour delay out of Heathrow Airport. One and a half hours due to fog - and one and a half hours due to a bomb scare! Not a good thing for a nervous traveller! Everyone got very tense, fearing not, as I was, the flight but that we would miss the concert! At last we made a safe touchdown in Dublin. It must have looked very funny to the airport staff, for suddenly the apparently almost empty building was invaded by a stampeding herd of Garth

Brooks' fans! We all ran through the terminal and virtually threw ourselves into the waiting taxis. We made it to the hotel with less than an hour in hand, and from there to the stadium.

The major set on this concert tour takes the form of a space ship. It is awe-inspiring, it really is. I had never seen anything like it. The space ship delivered the band onto the stage - but no Garth. The band prowled around the stage, heightening the already electric atmosphere by playing crescendos of music that made us all think that Garth was about to appear. Finally he did. I'm not going to tell you the form this appearance took because, as I have already said, Garth likes to surprise people and this tour is still in progress.

But, my God, the presence of the man! He's a powerhouse, able to lead the audience wherever he chooses with just a look or a gesture. I could hardly believe it was true - there he was - right in front of me! He's a big man, over six feet and built to match. He looked great - hard and lean - his fitness a by-product of the current tour. And no wonder. He had a catwalk running along in front of the stage, all 450 feet of it, and at times he would run from one end to the other and back, but still have enough breath to sing when he got there. I tried to soak everything up, knowing that if I didn't concentrate, it would all suddenly be over, and I'd only remember a blur.

So how did I feel, now that my dream of seeing him was fulfilled? It was very odd. I was stunned, mesmerised, by the energy of his performance. And incredibly proud of him when I saw the total unequivocal love that the audience had for him. But I could feel no trace of Ryan. None at all. The huge mega star persona left no room for anyone else. But, after all, Ryan was also very charismatic, so I waited for him to appear.

Garth's energy loop with the audience is amazing, and, as their excitement grew, he too grew crazier. At one point he even produced a skilful back-flip off a piece of scenery out of sheer exuberance. The stage was pounded with a steady stream of roses, gifts, and notes. Several ladies went to the edge of the stage and received a quick hug or kiss. At times Garth's legs could scarcely be seen beneath the forest of hands that clutched at him.

If only I had known the layout of the stadium, maybe I could have brought a ticket for the standing area which was far below me. As it was I was separated from it by a sheer drop - there was no way down.

He brought his wife Sandy on stage, and complained, laughingly, that we cheered more for her than him! It was lovely to see that, when Sandy became tearful at the strength of the audience's huge response to her, she naturally ran to Garth to be hugged by him.

Half way through the concert, things changed for the better, and for the worse, depending on how you looked at it. He was singing what for me has always been one of his most inspirational songs - *The Dance* - when something extraordinary happened. I had, strangely, always thought of this as Ryan's theme song. Garth stared up towards me intently, and I stared back, unblinking : transfixed - again. He walked forward a few steps, ignoring the grasping hands that reached for him, as the crowd grew excited once more. Even though he was some distance away, something passed between us. Then the people seemed to sense something magical taking place. Those nearest to me lowered their hands and fell silent. All I could hear were the words of *The Dance* spiralling up through the night air, crystalline in their clarity. What a voice! And for that time, for me, Garth was Ryan. These words were coming to me direct from Ryan. I didn't know how that could be - I just knew that it was true. Time seemed to stand still but in another sense it flew by. I felt every word that he sang deep inside my soul. I understood what it meant: that our past life was over: that there should be no regrets. *The Dance* is a song with a very clear meaning: that it is better to have loved and lost than never to have loved at all: that it's better to chase a dream, even if you fail, than to keep it as just that - a dream.

I certainly believe that it was worth all the pain I went through, as Madeleine, to know Ryan. I would not have missed knowing him for anything. And even had I known how it would end - it would still have been worth it.

As if God had flicked a switch, the sounds of the crowd filtered back into my hearing, that for a time had heard only his voice. The concert reappeared around me. I realised that there were silent tears streaming down my face. The rest of the concert was dream-like. I was in another world - another time. I was elated - and I was heartbroken. For right then, I was in torment. To have the soul that I loved, so near, and yet be unable to reach him, was like offering a crumb of bread to a starving man - almost worse than nothing. The pain of losing Ryan had eased but the pain of wanting to look into his eyes, up close - to hug him - remained. I walked back to the hotel in a daze. All the other fans were exultant - I was devastated.

The next morning I found out through an inside source which hotel Garth was staying at. I went there with two of my new friends. We met Sandy inside. She told us that Garth had left - through the very same door we had just used - ten minutes previously. Ten minutes! It obviously wasn't meant to be. Clearly, some spirit that knows better than me has decreed that the time is not right for me to talk to Garth face to face. Maybe this book needs to be published so that Garth can read it at his leisure, and choose to remember - or not - whatever is best for him. I have to accept it - for now. But the quest will go on - I could not stop even if I wanted to.

What does the future hold now? I will, I hope, become an established songwriter. Perhaps I will have some more regressions to relate. But, please remember, you can do this yourself. And in your current lifetime you might meet someone that you either really like or really hate at first sight. Next time this happens to you, consider; you may have a reason for this reaction. You may have known this person before.

I have been really fortunate in that this past-life soul-mate of mine is seen on TV in this life, otherwise I may never have rediscovered him; after all we do live on different continents - although I do believe it was meant to happen. Some people believe that soul-mates often cross our paths in order to steer us onto our right path. I really believe Garth has done this for me. I was definitely headed in the wrong direction - downhill.

I sit here now, gazing up at Ryan's portrait where it hangs above my PC and I feel very privileged. No-one can take my memories away from me now. I have also been made complete by Madeleine joining me, and I now have that all-important, strong sense of who I am, something which so many seem to lack. I also have another equally wonderful man to love me in this life, another soul-mate - so how lucky can one person be? Tony and I will walk into the future together, knowing that there is little to fear.

As for Garth; I hope one day to become a trusted friend. When I know him better, I may show him his story, and maybe one day I'll tell him that it's true. What his reaction may be I truly do not know. I have already had most of this story read by a friend of Garth's in Nashville. Her response was to say that she believed the story must be true. Her reason for saying this, was that she didn't think I could have portrayed Garth's character as Ryan so accurately unless I knew him very well too - and of course I don't, not yet anyway. So - I may get to speak to Garth any day now - who knows? My favourite maxim, after my experiences over the last three years is: 'You never know how your life might change in a minute.'

Epilogue

What do you think happened to Margaret? If I were you I would want to know. I certainly did. Eventually I got her maiden name; it was Beresford. She became insane when she was thirty-eight years old and lived the rest of her life that way: a fitting punishment, I think. But how did she go mad and why? Call it revenge if you like, or call it satisfaction but I wanted to know. So I called on my spirit-guide to show me. This is how I believe it happened.

Madeleine's father, Edwin, who had already been ill, died about six months after Madeleine's suicide. He finally saw, I think, how criminally foolish he had been. He had always known that Margaret's actions were cruel and sinful, but he could not find the strength to resist her. He knew that by his inaction he had caused the death, not only of Ryan but of Madeleine too. And in the end his conscience could not live with the guilt. I believe that is what killed him.

With his death, Margaret had it all, or so she thought. She had the house, the wealth, and the position of power that went with it. But she was alone, and after a few months, she hated it. None of the servants liked her, and she had no friends and no-one to talk to. It appeared that everyone except Edwin had finally seen through her civilised veneer and into her black heart. And now that Edwin was gone, his friends were gone too. At thirty-eight years of age, she was not yet old and she began to regret that she had only ever given herself to an old man who had left her a lonely widow. She regretted that she had never enjoyed the attention of a young or vigorous man, something she had never allowed herself because of her ambitions. She was often afraid at night, when quiet corners and hallways seemed to hold some hidden menace in their shadows. At these times she longed for someone strong to comfort her.

One night she had a nightmare. She could not remember it because she awoke to a terrible storm raging around the house and the dream fled in shreds before she could register it. She huddled, alone and miserable, beneath the covers of her bed, trembling with fear until the early dawn brought relief and peace.

The next night the dream returned. It centred around the dreadful storm when she had been lost in the woods and Ryan had saved her. This time, as before, she crouched at the base of the massive oak tree. But this time, as soon as his hands touched her, things changed and she knew it was he. And so this time as she turned and collapsed in his arms, she knew that it was Ryan who held her. When he pulled her close to his body she felt, to her horror and amazement, a sharp sexual thrill at his vital presence against her. And with it came the awful knowledge that she would never again feel this from any living man. She awoke at this thought, sweating and angry at her fickle mind for betraying her this way. She had never felt any attraction towards him, only hatred, always hatred. She scorned herself for this ridiculous dream.

But each night the dream returned until one night it went further. This time, as she sheltered in his embrace, she found herself reaching up and putting her arms around his neck. Then she kissed him. Now as their lips met, she finally felt real power, not the false power she had sought all her life which had left her empty and unhappy. Now some small clean corner of her mind tried to tell her what she had done, and her resistance to it wrenched her from the dream. It could not be true! It could not! She had loathed him at first sight. There had been no feeling of attraction - none!

And yet she found her fingertips tracing her lips in remembrance of his touch. She was furious with herself. But the dreams continued - she always forcing herself to wakefulness at that point, not letting the dream progress further, until she was almost afraid to sleep.

But one night her weariness was such that she could not awaken, and the dream held her fast. Once again she found herself relishing the feel of his body against hers, once again she kissed him. This time the kiss continued; it sent a shock right through to the centre of her being, and she knew this was desire. She wanted him. She had never before felt this need, never before experienced this passion. All her life she had used men - old men and love-making - only as a means of furthering her ambitions. She had never allowed herself to discover any other way. Now the dream shattered and when she awoke it was to the realisation that she never would experience this other, powerful way, and that she had made a dreadful mistake.

When the dream returned the next night she surrendered to it - and him. If this was all she could ever have then she would use it. Once more she was out in the storm but this time her mind was not centred on the terror of it; this time she waited hungrily for the sensation of his kiss to take her. As their lips met she allowed her emotions to run wild. With her hands entwined in his hair, she pulled him closer, closer until she felt out of control. This was the way a woman should feel. She realised that now and welcomed it, revelled in it. Let the dream go further, let Ryan take her - right there in the wet grass, in the height of the storm.

But suddenly it all went wrong. In an instant she felt him pull away sharply. In the dream she opened her eyes. He was looking down at her with disgust and loathing and total rejection. He did not want her! No! This was her dream and she would control it!

But she awoke, her bedclothes in disarray, her skin wet with sweat. Now she was furious with him once more. Even in a dream - even after death - still he thwarted her at every turn! She must feed her hate, drive him from her mind. But she could not. The dream returned as soon as she slept, and she could not awaken or change its course. Still he rejected her, pulling from her embrace and standing over her disdainfully. Suddenly the storm crashed back into her heart. Terror returned as once more she could feel the oak tree tremble in its wrath. Desperately she clung to Ryan's legs.

'Do not leave me!' she screamed. But before her eyes he shimmered and faded, and her hands closed on…nothing. The storm raged on and she tried to awaken, her heart skittering in her breast until she thought it would burst.

Finally, with a desperate cry, she tore herself from sleep and leapt from the bed, lest the dream claim her once more. She was drawn to the window, as if by invisible strings, and she stood there panting, trying to calm her body and her mind. She could see the barn from there, where he had slept. This was where she had spied on Madeleine during her visit to Ryan in the night. Then she had persuaded her husband to offer Ryan a bribe to leave, totally convinced that he would take it. When he had not she had been insanely angry, and determined to break him somehow; she had paid the men that had almost killed Ryan. But that too had failed! She had nevertheless gained a lot of satisfaction from seeing Ryan a few days later having to walk so carefully. Obviously the men had hurt him a great deal and, judging by the way he carried himself, he would remember the result of defying her for some time to come.

She tried to bind her thoughts to hatred of him, to remember an incident when she had been so angry she could have killed him with her bare hands. That would put paid to the dreams!

She had it! Late last summer; the last garden party she had held. He had seen to it that she could bear no more! Margaret was becoming incoherent now, as madness began to insinuate into her senses, so I was shown this incident through Madeleine's eyes, and she tells the tale.

'Today, Mother held a garden party. Ryan and I were instructed to keep well out of the way, and we did until - well, perhaps I should explain from the beginning. She liked to make fools of people. I supposed she gained a perverse kind of power from it. She had a really cruel streak in her that wallowed in someone else's misery. She would often invite one or two totally unsuitable couples to these events - fostering their belief that they had been accepted into the higher echelons of society but for the sole purpose of amusing her other guests. Their clothes would, of course, always point them out as objects of ridicule. But on this particular day that was not enough for her. She had hatched an evil plot with some of her cronies. When John and Monica Barrett, a well-meaning, kindly couple, arrived at the party their faces were shining with pride. They found, to their amazement, that they were fully accepted by everyone and they seemed to be meriting a flattering amount of attention.

'After an hour or so the plan was put into action. Mother turned them around, so that they were suddenly confronted by a very regal-looking man and woman who were dressed in fine silks and velvets. The man regarded the Barretts with disdainful expectation. Neither poor John nor his wife knew what was expected of them and they stood in total bewilderment. The foppish man was holding a lace handkerchief which he flicked from side to side as if in impatience. John and Monica could hear the crowd around them beginning to mutter and snigger but they had no idea of what they were to do.

'"M—my Lord?" John stammered, inquiringly.

'At this the man spoke angrily: "Do you not bow before your sovereign!" he demanded.

'"M—my God, the K—king!" John stuttered, "—your Highness—I beg your forgiveness!—I am so sorry!" The poor pair fell to their knees in mortification, their faces red. At this, the entire assemblage, including the 'king', who was of course not the king at all, broke into uproarious laughter. It took several moments before the Barretts discovered the plot and realised that they had been made into complete fools.

'Mother completed their discomfiture, by saying loudly, "Now perhaps you have learned not to try and stand amongst those who are your superiors! From now on stay with the common peasants where you belong!" The whole company laughed again and John and Monica could only flee in abject shame.

'In their hurry to escape they took a wrong turn and collided with Nancy at the kitchen door. By this time Monica was in tears and her husband was near to it.

'"My dears, my dears!" exclaimed Nancy. "Whatever is wrong?" They were incapable of speaking clearly so Nancy ushered them into the kitchen, her safe haven for all. Of course, Ryan and I were seated at the table, keeping out of Mother's way. After a while, when they could speak again, the whole sorry tale was recounted. As always when he was aroused, either in pleasure or in anger, I saw Ryan's eyes darken in colour and begin to glint dangerously. He was a very tolerant man and would normally stand a lot of goading, but as I have said before, the cruel antics of some of the rich folk incensed him beyond endurance. He stood up hurriedly, pushing his chair back with an aggressive shove, and he strode out of the back door without a word. Nancy and I looked at each other, no words necessary. When Ryan became like this even I could not stop him. He became reckless and totally uncaring of his own position.

'We all watched and listened from the back doorway. Mother did not notice Ryan at first, but gradually she realised that silence was descending over her yet mirthful guests as he pushed his way, none too gently between them, in order to reach her.

270

'"How dare you!" she screeched. "Get back to the servants' quarters where you belong!" She had never acknowledged Ryan as her son-in-law, and she certainly did not intend to do so there in front of all her high class friends. Ryan however had other plans. He looked very out of place in his rough shirt and plain breeches among all the strutting peacocks that adorned the gardens.

'He interrupted her before she could continue, "Ladies and gentlemen, it is my misfortune to have cause to call this lady - Mother."

'Gasps of amazement and glee could be heard all around, at this juicy piece of gossip.

'"And how dare you—" Ryan continued, "—treat decent people in this appalling way? They have done you no harm although, as I well know, that is not necessary in order to fall foul of your despicable behaviour. The Barretts may not be able to call themselves members of your high society, but they are more deserving members of the human race than all of you."

'Mother was flustered, and when she was thus her only recourse was to hit out. So she tried to slap Ryan in the face as she had once done before, but he caught her wrist and held it tightly.

'"No, " he said, "not again." She struggled but he would not let her loose.

'"Let me go!" she screamed, looking around her for support. But like a pack of jackals, they soon turned on their own in times of trouble. Besides, there was not one man enough to try and tackle Ryan in this mood. When he had held her long enough for her to understand that she would get no help from her friends, and that he had this power over her, he let her go with a quick disdainful flick and turned to walk back to the kitchen.

'That might have been the end of it, except that standing next to the ornamental pond and fountain was the man who had played the part of the king. It was too easy for Ryan and he could not resist. As he came abreast of the man he turned and bowed in mock humility.

'"Your Majesty!" he said, and in one swift movement he barrelled into the "king" at waist height, and tossed him over the wall and into the pond. With a startled shriek the pretender floundered on his back in the water in complete panic. Without a backward glance, Ryan returned to the back door. Now it was John and Monica's turn to laugh, and I laughed too. But beneath this I was truly concerned. Ryan did himself no good at all by antagonising Mother in this way. But he was only being himself and, as I loved him to his very soul, I would not have him any other way.'

* * *

As she relived this memory Margaret felt her hatred blossoming once more. He had made a complete fool of her in front of everyone that mattered. Her position in the community had been damaged beyond redemption. So once more she relished the thought of his pain. She held on to thoughts of how badly the men in her pay had hurt him and it comforted her. She did hate him, she truly hated him with every fibre of her being - and yet - she shivered involuntarily as she remembered the feeling of his hands on her skin. She longed to feel those hands once more; such strong, assured hands travelling over her body - to feel his mouth - No! No! It was not true! She would not let it be true! In any case he

272

was dead. They had finally found out for sure. Every one of his party had been slaughtered. The body that her dream tried to tell her she wanted lay in a shallow unmarked grave near Lumley Castle where he had fallen. Margaret had even insisted that his bloody remains were identified - to be sure. She stared out into the darkness. She was so alone and afraid - afraid even of her own mind which seemed to have turned against her.

She caught a sudden flash of white out in the moonlight. She stared. She felt sure she could make out the tall figure of a man staring up at her window. She could see his white shirt billowing in the wind. She gasped. Terror seized her heart, forcing it up into her throat. No! No! It could not be! But she could see the figure clearly now. As the moonlight struck him, she could see that the front of his shirt was heavily stained with blood, looking black in the silver light. Now his face was clearly lit and, even as her mind was tumbling - down and down into a dark pit within her - she still recognised those eyes. Despite the distance between his eyes and hers she could still feel them burning like fire. She swooned and fell to the floor.

When she awoke in the dawn she had aged ten years. Within days she had moved out of the house and into a nearby cottage where darkness ceased to exist - for there were candles burning all through the night in every single room. She became a recluse. She lived the remainder of her life in an imaginary twilight world of dread. She knew, I think, that the worst of her punishment lay ahead of her.

The End